GREENFIELD HILL

AMS PRESS
NEW YORK

GREENFIELD HILL:

A

POEM,

IN

SEVEN PARTS.

BY TIMOTHY DWIGHT, D. D.

NEW-YORK;—PRINTED BY CHILDS AND SWAINE.
1794.

*In this reprint, the original pagination
has been maintained*

Reprinted from the edition of 1794
First AMS EDITION published 1970
Manufactured in the United States of America

International Standard Book Number: 0-404-02227-8

Library of Congress Catalog Number: 73-144600

811.2
D993g

AMS PRESS INC.
NEW YORK, N.Y. 10003

To JOHN ADAMS, Efquire,

VICE-PRESIDENT OF THE UNITED STATES
OF AMERICA,

THIS Poem is infcribed with Sentiments of the
higheft Refpect for his Private Character, and
for the important Services he has rendered
his Country,

By his very Obedient,

And Moft humble Servant,

TIMOTHY DWIGHT.

THE INTRODUCTION.

IN the Parish of Greenfield, in the Town of Fair-
field, in Connecticut, there is a pleasant and beautiful
eminence, called Greenfield Hill; at the distance of
three miles from Long-Island Sound. On this emi-
nence, there is a small but handsome Village, a Church,
Academy, &c. all of them alluded to in the following
Poem. From the highest part of the eminence, the
eye is presented with an extensive and delightful
prospect of the surrounding Country, and of the
Sound. On this height, the Writer is supposed to
stand. The First object, there offering itself to his
view, is the Landscape; which is accordingly made
the governing subject of the First Part of the Poem.
The flourishing and happy condition of the Inhabit-
ants very naturally suggested itself next; and became
of course, the subject of the Second Part. The
Town of Fairfield, lying in full view, and, not long
before the Poem was begun, and in a great measure
written out, burnt by a party of British Troops,
under the command of Governor Tryon, furnished
the theme of the Third Part. A Field, called the

Pequod Swamp, in which, moſt of the warriors of that nation, who ſurvived the invaſion of their country by Capt. Maſon, were deſtroyed, lying about three miles from the eminence abovementioned, and on the margin of the Sound, ſuggeſted not unnaturally, the ſubjeƈt of the Fourth Part.

As the writer is the Miniſter of Greenfield, he cannot be ſuppoſed to be unintereſted in the welfare of his Pariſhioners. To excite their attention to the truths and duties of Religion (an objeƈt in ſuch a ſituation, inſtinƈtively riſing to his view,) is the deſign of the Fifth Part; And to promote in them juſt ſentiments and uſeful conduƈt, for the preſent life, (an objeƈt cloſely conneƈted with the preceding one) of the Sixth.

Many of the ſubjeƈts, mentioned in the Poem, and ſuggeſted by the general ſtate of this Country, eaſily led a contemplative mind to look forward, and call up to view its probable ſituation at a diſtant approaching period. The ſolid foundations, which appear to be laid for the future greatneſs and proſperity of the American Republic, offered very pleaſing views of this ſubjeƈt to a Poet; and of theſe the writer has, in the Seventh Part of the Work, endeavoured to avail himſelf.

To contribute to the innocent amuſement of his countrymen, and to their improvement in manners, and in œconomical, political, and moral ſentiments, is the object which the writer wiſhes to accompliſh. As he is firmly perſuaded, that his countrymen are furniſhed by Providence with as extenſive and advantageous means of proſperity, as the world has hitherto ſeen, ſo he thinks it the duty and the intereſt of every citizen, to promote it, by all the means in his power. Poetry appears to him to be one, among the probable means of advancing this purpoſe. " Allow me to make the Songs of a nation," ſaid a wiſe man, "and who will may make their Laws." Poetry may not, perhaps, produce greater effects in promoting the proſperity of mankind, than philoſophy;* but the effects which it produces, are far from being ſmall. Where truth requires little illuſtration, and only needs to be ſet in a ſtrong and affecting light, Poetry appears to be as advantageous an inſtrument of making uſeful impreſſions, as can be eaſily conceived. It will be read by many perſons, who would ſcarcely look at a logical diſcuſſion; by moſt readers it will be more deeply felt, and more laſtingly remembered; and, to ſay the leaſt, it will, in the preſent caſe, be an unuſual, and for that reaſon may be a forcible method of treating ſeveral ſubjects, handled in this Poem.

When the writer began the work, he had no deſign of publiſhing it; aiming merely to amuſe his own mind, and to gain a temporary relief from the

* See Lowth's Lectures on Heb. Po.

preſſure of melancholy. Hence it was dropped, at an early period; when other avocations, or amuſements preſented themſelves. The greater part of it was written ſeven years ago. Additions have been made to it, at different periods, from that time to the preſent—This will account for the dates of ſeveral things mentioned in it, which would otherwiſe ſeem to be improperly connected.

Originally the writer deſigned to imitate, in the ſeveral parts, the manner of as many Britiſh Poets; but finding himſelf too much occupied, when he projected the publication, to purſue that deſign, he relinquiſhed it. The little appearance of ſuch a deſign, ſtill remaining, was the reſult of diſtant and general recollection. Much, of that nature, he has rejected, and all he would have rejected, had not even that rejection demanded more time than he could afford for ſuch a purpoſe. Theſe facts will, he hopes, apologize to the reader, for the mixed manner which he may, at times, obſerve in the performance.

Greenfield, June 13th, 1794.

GREENFIELD HILL:

A

POEM.

THE ARGUMENT.

SPRING—*General Prospect*—*View of the Inland Country*—*Of the beauty of Vegetation at the time of Harvest*—*Of the happy state of the Inhabitants*—*Men esteemed in New-England according to their personal qualities*—*State of New-England*—*Connecticut*—*State of Society in Europe contrasted to that of New-England*—*People of New-England exhorted not to copy the Government, Manners, &c. of other nations*—*Remembrance of the late Councils and Armies of the United States*—*Prospect of the Country between Greenfield Hill and the Sound*—*Description of the Sound*—*Retrospect of the troubles occasioned by the British Marauding Parties*—*Wish for perpetual Peace*—*Beauty of the Scenes of Nature*—*Happiness of a Clergyman in the Country*—*Address to the Clergy.*

GREENFIELD HILL.

PART I.

THE PROSPECT.

FROM fouthern ifles, on winds of gentleft wing,
Sprinkled with morning dew, and rob'd in green,
Life in her eye, and mufic in her voice,
Lo Spring returns, and wakes the world to joy!
Forth creep the fmiling herbs; expand the flowers;   5
New-loos'd, and burfting from their icy bonds,
The ftreams frefh-warble, and through every mead
Convey reviving verdure; every bough,
Full-blown and lovely, teems with fweets and fongs;
And hills, and plains, and paftures feel the prime.   10

     As round me here I gaze, what profpects rife?
Etherial! matchlefs! fuch as Albion's fons,
Could Albion's ifle an equal profpect boaft,
In all the harmony of numerous fong,
Had tun'd to rapture, and o'er Cooper's hill,   15
And Windfor's beauteous foreft, high uprais'd,
And fent on fame's light wing to every clime.
Far inland, blended groves, and azure hills,
Skirting the broad horizon, lift their pride.
Beyond, a little chafm to view unfolds   20
Cerulean mountains, verging high on Heaven,
In mifty grandeur. Stretch'd in nearer view,
Unnumber'd farms falute the cheerful eye;
Contracted there to little gardens; here outfpread

Spacious, with paſtures, fields, and meadows rich; 25
Where the young wheat it's glowing green diſplays,
Or the dark ſoil beſpeaks the recent plough,
Or flocks and herds along the lawn diſport.

Fair is the landſchape ; but a fairer ſtill 30
Shall ſoon inchant the ſoul—when harveſt full
Waves wide its bending wealth. Delightful taſk !
To trace along the rich, enamell'd ground,
The ſweetly varied hues ; from India's corn,
Whoſe black'ning verdure bodes a bounteous crop,
Through lighter graſs, and lighter ſtill the flax, 35
The paler oats, the yellowiſh barley, wheat
In golden glow, and rye in brighter gold.
Theſe ſoon the ſight ſhall bleſs. Now other ſcenes
The heart dilate, where round, in rural pride
The village ſpreads its tidy, ſnug retreats, 40
That ſpeak the induſtry of every hand.

How bleſs'd the ſight of ſuch a numerous train
In ſuch ſmall limits, taſting every good
Of competence, of independence, peace,
And liberty unmingled ; every houſe 45
On its own ground, and every happy ſwain
Beholding no ſuperior, but the laws,
And ſuch as virtue, knowledge, uſeful life,
And zeal, exerted for the public good,
Have rais'd above the throng. For here, in truth, 50
Not in pretence, man is eſteem'd as man.
Not here how rich, of what peculiar blood,
Or office high ; but of what genuine worth,
What talents bright and uſeful, what good deeds,
What piety to God, what love to man, 55
The queſtion is. To this an anſwer fair
The general heart ſecures. Full many a rich,
Vile knave, full many a blockhead, proud
Of ancient blood, theſe eyes have ſeen float down

Life's dirty kennel, trampled in the mud,   60
Stepp'd o'er unheeded, or pufh'd rudely on;
While Merit, rifing from her humble fkiff
To barks of nobler, and ftill nobler fize,
Sail'd down the expanding ftream, in triumph gay,
By every fhip faluted.   65

             Hail, O hail
My much-lov'd native land! New Albion hail!
The happieft realm, that, round his circling courfe,
The all-fearching fun beholds. What though the breath
Of Zembla's winter fhuts thy lucid ftreams,   70
And hardens into brafs thy generous foil;
Though, with one white, and cheerlefs robe, thy hills,
Invefted, rife a long and joylefs wafte;
Leaflefs the grove, and dumb the lonely fpray,
And every pafture mute: What though with clear   75
And fervid blaze, thy fummer rolls his car,
And drives the languid herd, and fainting flock
To feek the fhrouding umbrage of the dale;
While Man, relax'd and feeble, anxious waits
The dewy eve, to flake his thirfty frame: 80
What though thy furface, rocky, rough, and rude,
Scoop'd into vales, or heav'd in lofty hills,
Or cloud-embofom'd mountains, dares the plough,
And threatens toil intenfe to every fwain:
What though foul Calumny, with voice malign,   85
Thy generous fons, with every virtue grac'd,
Accus'd of every crime, and ftill rolls down
The kennell'd ftream of impudent abufe:
Yet to high HEAVEN my ardent praifes rife,
That in thy lightfome vales he gave me birth,   90
All-gracious, and allows me ftill to live.

    Cold is thy clime, but every weftern blaft
Brings health, and life, and vigour on his wings;
Innerves the fteely frame, and firms the foul

With ſtrength and hardihood; wakes each bold   95
And manly purpóſe; bears above the ills,
That ſtretch, upon the rack, the languid heart
Of ſummer's maiden ſons, in pleaſure's lap,
Dandled to dull repoſe.   Exertion ſtrong
Marks their whole life.   Mountains before them ſink   100
To mole-hills; oceans bar their courſe in vain.
Thro' the keen wintry wind they breaſt their way,
Or ſummer's fierceſt flame.   Dread dangers rouſe
Their hearts to pleaſing conflict; toils and woes,
Quicken their ardour: while, in milder climes,   105
Their peers effeminate they ſee, with ſcorn
On lazy plains, diſſolv'd in putrid ſloth,
And ſtruggling hard for being.   Thy rough ſoil
Tempts hardy labour, with his ſturdy team,
To turn, with ſinewy hand, the ſtony glebe,   110
And call forth every comfort from the mould,
Unpromiſing, but kind.   Thy houſes, barns,
Thy granaries, and thy cellars, hence are ſtor'd
With all the ſweets of life: while, thro' thy realm,
A native beggar rarely pains the ſight.   115

    Thy ſummer glows with heat; but choiceſt fruits
Hence purple in the ſun; hence ſparkling flowers
Gem the rich landſchape; double harveſts hence
Load the full fields: pale Famine ſcowls aloof,
And Plenty wantons round thy varied year.   120

    Rough is thy ſurface; but each landſchape bright,
With all of beauty, all of grandeur dreſs'd,
Of mountains, hills, and ſweetly winding vales,
Of foreſts, groves, and lawns, and meadows green,
And waters, varied by the plaſtic hand,   125
Through all their fairy ſplendour, ceaſeleſs charms,
Poetic eyes.   Springs bubbling round the year,
Gay-wand'ring brooks, wells at the ſurface full,
Yield life, and health, and joy, to every houſe,

And every vivid field. Rivers, with foamy courfe,   130
Pour o'er the ragged cliff the white cafcade,
And roll unnumber'd mills; or, like the Nile,
Fatten the beauteous interval; or bear
The fails of commerce through the laughing groves.

With wifdom, virtue, and the generous love   135
Of learning, fraught, and freedom's living flame,
Electric, unextinguifhable, fir'd,
Our Sires eftablifhed, in thy cheerful bounds,
The nobleft inftitutions, man has feen,
Since time his reign began. In little farms   140
They meafur'd all thy realms, to every child
In equal fhares defcending; no entail
The firft-born lifting into bloated pomp,
Tainting with luft, and floth, and pride, and rage,
The world around him : all the race befide,   145
Like brood of oftrich, left for chance to rear,
And every foot, to trample. Reafon's fway
Elective, founded on the rock of truth,
Wifdom their guide, and equal good their end,
They built with ftrength, that mocks the battering ftorm,   150
And fpurns the mining flood; and every right
Difpens'd alike to all. Beneath their eye,
And forming hand, in every hamlet, rofe
The nurturing fchool; in every village, fmil'd
The heav'n-inviting church, and every town   155
A world within itfelf, with order, peace,
And harmony, adjufted all its weal.

Hence every fwain, free, happy, his own lord,
With ufeful knowledge fraught, of bufinefs, laws,
Morals, religion, life, unaw'd by man,   160
And doing all, but ill, his heart can wifh,
Looks round, and finds ftrange happinefs his own;
And fees that happinefs on laws depend.
On this heav'n-laid foundation refts thy fway;

On knowledge to difcern, and fenfe to feel, 165
That free-born rule is life's perennial fpring
Of real good. On this alone it refts.
For, could thy fons a full conviction feel,
That government was noxious, without arms,
Without intrigues, without a civil broil, 170
As torrents fweep the fand-built ftructure down,
A vote would wipe it's very trace away.
Hence too each breaft is fteel'd for bold defence;
For each has much to lofe. Chofen by all,
The meffenger of peace, by all belov'd, 175
Spreads, hence, the truth and virtue, he commands.
Hence manners mild, and fweet, their peaceful fway
Widely extend. Refinement of the heart
Illumes the general mafs. Even thofe rude hills,
Thofe deep embow'ring woods, in other lands 180
Prowl'd round by favages, the fame foft fcenes,
Mild manners, order, virtue, peace, difclofe;
The howling foreft polifh'd as the plain.

From earlieft years, the fame enlightened foul
Founded bright fchools of fcience. Here the mind 185
Learn'd to expand it's wing, and ftretch it's flight
Through truth's broad fields. Divines, and lawyers, hence,
Phyficians, ftatefmen, all with wifdom fraught,
And learning, fuited to the ufe of life,
And minds, by bufinefs, fharpen'd into fenfe, ·190
Sagacious of the duty, and the weal,
Of man, fpring numberlefs; and knowledge hence
Pours it's falubrious ftreams, through all the fpheres
Of human life. Its bounds, and generous fcope,
Hence Education opens, fpreading far 195
Through the bold yeomanry, that fill thy climes,
Views more expanded, generous, juft, refin'd,
Than other nations know. In other lands,
The mafs of man, fcarce rais'd above the brutes,

Drags dull the horfemill round of fluggifh life :   200
Nought known, beyond their daily toil ; all elfe
By ignorance' dark curtain hid from fight.
Here, glorious contraft ! every mind, infpir'd
With active inquifition, reftlefs wings
Its flight to every flower, and, fettling, drinks   205
Largely the fweets of knowledge.

                  Candour, fay,
Is this a ftate of life, thy honeft tongue
Could blacken ? Thefe a race of men, thy page
Could hand to infamy ? The fhameful tafk   210
Thy foes at firft began, and ftill thy foes,
Laborious, weave the web of lies. 'Tis hence
The generous traveller round him looks, amaz'd,
And wonders at our unexpected blifs.

    But chief, Connecticut! on thy fair breaft   215
Thefe fplendours glow. A rich improvement fmiles
Around thy lovely borders; in thy fields
And all that in thy fields delighted dwell.
Here that pure, golden mean, fo oft of yore
By fages wifh'd, and prais'd, by Agur's voice   220
Implor'd, while God th' approving fanction gave
Of wifdom infinite ; that golden mean,
Shines unalloy'd ; and here the extended good,
That mean alone fecures, is ceafelefs found.

    Oh, would fome faithful, wife, laborious mind,   225
Develope all thy fprings of blifs to man ;
Soon would politic vifions fleet away,
Before awakening truth ! Utopias then,
Ancient and new, high fraught with fairy good,
Would catch no more the heart. Philofophy   230
Would bow to common-fenfe; and man, from facts,
And real life, politic wifdom learn.

C

Ah then, thou favour'd land, thyfelf revere!
Look not to Europe, for examples juft
Of order, manners, cuftoms, doctrines, laws,   235
Of happinefs, or virtue. Caft around
The eye of fearching reafon, and declare
What Europe proffers, but a patchwork fway;
The garment Gothic, worn to fritter'd fhreds,
And eked from every loom of following times.   240
Such as his fway, the fyftem fhows entire,
Of filly pomp, and meannefs train'd t' adore;
Of wealth enormous, and enormous want;
Of lazy finecures, and fuffering toil;
Of grey-beard-fyftems, and meteorous dreams;   245
Of lordly churches, and diffention fierce,
Rites farfical, and phrenzied unbelief.
See thick and fell her lowering gibbets ftand,
And gibbets ftill employ'd! while, through thy realms,
The rare-feen felon ftartles every mind   250
And fills each mouth with news. Behold her jails
Countlefs, and ftow'd with wretches of all kinds!
Her brothels, circling, with their tainted walls,
Unnumber'd female outcafts, fhorne from life,
Peace, penitence, and hope; and down, down plung'd 255
In vice' unbottom'd gulph! Ye demons, rife,
Rife, and look upward, from your dread abode;
And, if you've tears to fhed, diftil them here!
See too, in countlefs herds, the miftrefs vile,
Even to the teeth of matron fanctity,   260
Lift up her fhamelefs bronze, and elbow out
The pure, the chafte, the lovely angel-form
Of female excellence! while leachers rank, and
Bloated, call aloud on vengeance' worms,
To feize their prey, on this fide of the grave.   265
See the foul theatre, with Upaz fteams,
Impoifoning half mankind! See every heart
And head from dunghills up to thrones, moon'd high

With fafhion, frippery, falling humbly down
To a new head-drefs ; barbers, milliners,   270
Taylors, and mantua-makers, forming gods,
Their fellow-millions worfhip ! See the world
All fet to fale ; truth, friendfhip, public truft,
A nation's weal, religion, fcripture, oaths,
Struck off by inch of candle ! Mark the mien,   275
Out-changing the Cameleon ; pleafing all,
And all deceiving ! Mark the fnaky tongue,
Now lightly vibrating, now hiffing death !
See war, from year to year, from age to age,
Unceafing, open on mankind the gates   280
Of devaftation ; earth wet-deep with blood,
And pav'd with corpfes ; cities whelm'd in flames ;
And fathers, brothers, hufbands, fons, and friends,
In millions hurried to th' untimely tomb ;
To gain a wigwam, built on Nootka Sound,   285
Or Falkland's fruitful ifles ; or to fecure
That rare foap-bubble, blown by children wife,
Bloated in air, and ting'd with colours fine,
Purfu'd by thoufands, and with rapture nam'd
National honour. But what powers fuffice   290
To tell the fands, that form the endlefs beach,
Or drops, that fill the immeafurable deep.

    Say then, ah fay, would'ft thou for thefe exchange
Thy facred inftitutions ? thy mild laws ?
Thy pure religion ? morals uncorrupt ?   295
Thy plain and honeft manners ? order, peace,
And general weal ? Think whence this weal arofe.
From the fame fprings it ftill fhall ceafelefs rife.
Preferve the fountains fweet, and fweeteft ftreams
Shall ftill flow from them. Change, but change alone,   300
By wife improvement of thy bleffings rare ;
And copy not from others. Shun the lures
Of Europe. Cherifh ftill, watch, hold,

And hold through every trial, every fnare,
All that is thine. Amend, refine, complete ;   305
But ftill the glorious ftamina retain.
Still, as of yore, in church, and ftate, elect
The virtuous, and the wife ; men tried, and prov'd,
Of fteady virtue, all thy weal to guide ;
And HEAVEN fhall blefs thee, with a parent's hand.   310

When round I turn my raptur'd eyes, with joy
O'erflowing, and thy wonderous blifs furvey,
I love to think of thofe, by whom that blifs
Was purchas'd ; thofe firm councils, that brave band,
Who nobly jeoparded their lives, their all,   315
And crofs'd temptation's whirlpool, to fecure,
For us, and ours, this rich eftate of good.
Ye fouls illuftrious, who, in danger's field,
Inftinct with patriot fire, each terror brav'd ;
And fix'd as thefe firm hills, the fhock withftood   320
Of war's convulfing earthquake, unappall'd,
Whilft on your labours gaz'd, with reverent eyes,
The pleas'd and wondering world ; let every good,
Life knows, let peace, efteem, domeftic blifs,
Approving confcience, and a grateful land,   325
Glory through every age, and Heaven at laft,
To crown the fplendid fcene, your toils reward.

Heavens, what a matchlefs group of beauties rare
Southward expands ! where, crown'd with yon tall oak,
Round-hill the circling land and fea o'erlooks ;   330
Or, fmoothly floping, Grover's beauteous rife,
Spreads it's green fides, and lifts its fingle tree,
Glad mark for feamen ; or, with ruder face,
Orchards, and fields, and groves, and houfes rare,
And fcatter'd cedars, Mill-hill meets the eye ;   335
Or where, beyond, with every beauty clad,
More diftant heights in vernal pride afcend.
On either fide, a long, continued range,

In all the charms of rural nature drefs'd,
Slopes gently to the main.　Ere Tryon funk　　340
To infamy unfathom'd, thro' yon groves
Once glifter'd Norwalk's white-afcending fpires,
And foon, if HEAVEN permit, fhall fhine again.
Here, fky-encircled, Stratford's churches beam;
And Stratfield's turrets greet the roving eye.　345
In clear, full view, with every varied charm,
That forms the finifh'd landfchape, blending foft
In matchlefs union, Fairfield and Green's Farms
Give luftre to the day.　Here, crown'd with pines
And fkirting groves, with creeks and havens fair　350
Embellifh'd, fed with many a beauteous ftream,
Prince of the waves, and ocean's favorite child,
Far weftward fading in confufion blue,
And eaftward ftretch'd beyond the human ken,
And mingled with the fky, there Longa's Sound　355
Glorious expands.　All hail! of waters firft
In beauties of all kinds; in profpects rich
Of bays, and arms, and groves, and little ftreams,
Inchanting capes and ifles, and rivers broad,
That yield eternal tribute to thy wave!　　360
In ufe fupreme : fifh of all kinds, all taftes,
Scaly or fhell'd, with floating nations fill
Thy fpacious realms; while, o'er thy lucid waves,
Unceafing Commerce wings her countlefs fails.
Safe in thy arms, the treafure moves along,　365
While, beat by Longa's coaft, old ocean roars
Diftant, but roars in vain.　O'er all thy bounds,
What varied beauties, changing with the fun,
Or night's more lovely queen, here fplendid glow.
Oft, on thy eaftern wave, the orb of light　370
Refulgent rifing, kindles wide a field
Of mimic day, flow failing to the weft,
And fading with the eve; and oft, through clouds,
Painting their dark fkirts on the glaffy plain,

The ftrong, pervading luftre marks th' expanfe,   375
With ftreaks of glowing filver, or with fpots
Of burnifh'd goid ; while clouds, of every hue,
Their purple fhed, their amber, yellow, grey,
Along the faithful mirror.   Oft, at eve,
Thron'd in the eaftern fky, th' afcending moon,   380
Diftain'd with blood, fits awful o'er the wave,
And, from the dim dark waters, troubled calls
Her dreary image, trembling on the deep,
And boding every horror.   Round yon ifles,
Where every Triton, every Nereid, borne   385
From eaftern climes, would find perpetual home,
Were Grecian fables true, what charms intrancè
The fafcinated eye ! where, half withdrawn
Behind yon vivid flope, like blufhing maids,
They leave the raptur'd gaze.   And O how fair   390
Bright Longa fpreads her terminating fhore,
Commix'd with whit'ning cliffs, with groves obfcure,
Farms fhrunk to garden-beds, and forefts fallen
To little orchards, flow-afcending hills,
And dufky vales, and plains ! Thefe the pleas'd eye   395
Relieve, engage, delight ; with one unchang'd,
Unbounded ocean, wearied, and difpleas'd.

Yet fcarce fix funs are pafs'd, fince thefe wide bounds,
So ftill fo lovely now, were wanton'd o'er
By fails of Britifh foes, with thunders dread   400
Announcing defolation to each field,
Each town, and hamlet ; in the fheltering night
Wafting bafe throngs of plunderers to our coaft,
The bed of peace invading ; herds and flocks
Purloining from the fwain ; and oft the houfe   405
Of innocence and peace, in cruel flames
With fell revenge, encircling.   Now, afar
With fhame retir'd, his bands no more, no more
(And oh may HEAVEN the fond prediction feal)

Shall hoftile bands, from earth's extended bounds,   410
Th' infernal talk refume. Henceforth, through time,
To peace devoted, 'till millenian funs
Call forth returning Eden, arts of peace
Shall triumph here. Speed, oh fpeed, ye days
Of blifs divine! when all-involving Heaven,   415
The myftery finifh'd, come the fecond birth
Of this fin-ruin'd, this apoftate world,
And clos'd the final fcene of wild mifrule,
All climes fhall clothe again with life, and joy,
With peace, and purity; and deathlefs fpring   420
Again commence her bright, etherial reign.

O who can paint, like Nature? who can boaft
Such fcenes, as here inchant the lingering eye?
Still to thy hand, great parent of the year!
I turn obfequious; ftill to all thy works   425
Of beauty, grandeur, novelty, and power,
Of motion, light, and life, my beating heart
Plays unifon; and, with harmonious thrill,
Inhales fuch joys,. as Avarice never knew.

Ah! knew he but his happinefs, of men   430
Not the leaft happy he, who, free from broils,
And bafe ambition, vain and buft'ling pomp,
Amid a friendly cure, and competence,
Taftes the pure pleafures of parochial life.
What though no crowd of clients, at his gate,   435
To falfhood, and injuftice, bribe his tongue,
And flatter into guilt; what though no bright,
And gilded profpects lure ambition on
To legiflative pride, or chair of ftate;
What though no golden dreams entice his mind   440
To burrow, with the mole, in dirt, and mire;
What though no fplendid villa, Eden'd round
With gardens of enchantment, walks of ftate,
And all the grandeur of fuperfluous wealth,

Invite the paffenger to ftay his fteed,   445
And afk the liveried foot-boy, " who dwells here ?"
What though no fwarms, around his fumptuous board,
Of foothing flatterers, humming in the fhine
Of opulence, and honey, from its flowers,
Devouring, 'till their time arrives to fting,   450
Inflate his mind; his virtues, round the year,
Repeating, and his faults, with microfcope
Inverted, leffen, 'till they fteal from fight:
Yet, from the dire temptations, thefe prefent,
His ftate is free ; temptations, few can ftem ;   455
Temptations, by whofe fweeping torrent hurl'd
Down the dire fteep of guilt, unceafing fall,
Sad victims, thoufands of the brighteft minds,
That time's dark reign adorn; minds, to whofe grafp
Heaven feems moft freely offer'd ; to man's eye,   460
Moft hopeful candidates for angels' joys.

   His lot, that wealth, and power, and pride forbids,
Forbids him to become the tool of fraud,
Injuftice, mifery, ruin ; faves his foul
From all the needlefs labours, griefs, and cares,   465
That avarice, and ambition, agonize;
From thofe cold nerves of wealth, that, palfied, feel
No anguifh, but its own ; and ceafelefs lead
To thoufand meanneffes, as gain allures.

   Though oft compell'd to meet the grofs attack   470
Of fhamelefs ridicule, and towering pride,
Sufficient good is his; good, real, pure,
With guilt unmingled.   Rarely forc'd from home,
Around his board, his wife and children fmile ;
Communion fweeteft, nature here can give,   475
Each fond endearment, office of delight,
With love and duty blending.   Such the joy,
My bofom oft has known.   His, too, the tafk,
To rear the infant plants, that bud around ;

To ope their little minds to truth's pure light;   480
To take them by the hand, and lead them on,
In that ftraight, narrow road, where virtue walks;
To guard them from a vain, deceiving world;
And point their courfe to realms of promis'd life.

His too th' efteem of thofe, who weekly hear   485
His words of truth divine; unnumber'd acts
Of real love attefting, to his eye,
Their filial tendernefs. Where'er he walks,
The friendly welcome and inviting fmile
Wait on his fteps, and breathe a kindred joy.   490

Oft too in friendlieft Affociation join'd,
He greets his brethren, with a flowing heart,
Flowing with virtue; all rejòic'd to meet,
And all reluctant parting; every aim,
Benevolent, aiding with purpofe kind;   495
While, feafon'd with unblemifh'd cheerfulnefs,
Far diftant from the tainted mirth of vice,
Their hearts difclofe each contemplation fweet
Of things divine; and blend in friendfhip pure,
Friendfhip fublim'd by piety and love.   500

All virtue's friends are his: the good, the juft,
The pious, to his houfe their vifits pay,
And converfe high hold of the true, the fair,
The wonderful, the moral, the divine:
Of faints, and prophets, patterns bright of truth,   505
Lent to a world of fin, to teach mankind,
How virtue, in that world, can live, and fhine;
Of learning's varied realms; of Nature's works;
And that blefs'd book, which gilds man's darkfome way,
With light from heaven; of blefs'd Meffiah's throne   510
And kingdom; prophefies divine fulfill'd,
And prophefies more glorious, yet to come,
In renovated days; of that bright world,

D

And all the happy trains, which that bright world
Inhabit, whither virtue's fons are gone :⠀⠀⠀⠀⠀⠀515
While God the whole infpires, adorns, exalts,
The fource, the end, the fubftance, and the foul.

This too the tafk, the blefs'd, the ufeful tafk,
To' invigour order, juftice, law, and rule ;
Peace to extend, and bid contention ceafe ;⠀⠀⠀520
To teach the words of life ; to lead mankind
Back from the wild of guilt, and brink of woe,
To virtue's houfe and family ; faith, hope,
And joy, t' infpire ; to warm the foul,
With love to God, and man ; to cheer the fad,⠀⠀525
To fix the doubting, roufe the languid heart ;
The wandering to reftore ; to fpread with down,
The thorny bed of death ; confole the poor,
Departing mind, and aid its lingering wing.

To him, her choiceft pages Truth expands,⠀⠀⠀⠀530
Uneeafing, where the foul-intrancing fcenes,
Poetic fiction boafts, are real all :
Where beauty, novelty, and grandeur, wear
Superior charms, and moral worlds unfold
Sublimities, tranfporting and divine.⠀⠀⠀⠀⠀⠀535

Not all the fcenes, Philofophy can boaft,
Tho' them with nobler truths he ceafelefs blends,
Compare with thefe. They, as they found the mind,
Still leave it ; more inform'd, but not more wife.
Thefe wifer, nobler, better, make the man.⠀⠀⠀540

Thus every happy mean of folid good
His life, his ftudies, and profeffion yield.
With motives hourly new, each rolling day,
Allures, through wifdom's path, and truth's fair field,
His feet to yonder fkies. Before him heaven⠀⠀⠀545
Shines bright, the fcope fublime of all his prayers,
The meed of every forrow, pain, and toil.

Then, O ye happy few! whom GOD allows
To ftand his meffengers, in this bad world,
And call mankind to virtue, weep no more,   550
Though pains and toils betide you : for what life,
On earth, from pains and toils was ever free ?
When Wealth and Pride around you gaily fpread
Their vain and tranfient fplendour, envy not.
How oft ('let virtue weep !) is this their all ?   555
For you, in funny profpect, daily fpring
Joys, which nor Pride can Tafte, nor Wealth can boaft ;
That, planted here, beyond the wintery grave
Revive and grow with ever vernal bloom.

Hail thefe, oh hail! and be 't enough for you,   560
To 'fcape a world unclean ; a life to lead
Of ufefulnefs, and truth ; a Prince to ferve,
Who fuffers no fincere and humble toil
To mifs a rich reward ; in Death's dark vale,
To meet unbofom'd light ; beyond the grave   565
To rife triumphant, freed from every ftain,
And cloth'd with every beauty ; in the fky
Stars to outfhine ; and, round th' eternal year,
With faints, with angels, and with CHRIST, to reign.

END OF THE FIRST PART.

GREENFIELD HILL:

A

P O E M.

THE ARGUMENT.

VIEW of the Village invested with the pleasing appearances of Spring—Recollection of the Winter—Pleasures of Winter—Of Nature and humble life—March—Original subject resumed—Freedom of the Villagers from manorial evils—Address to Competence, reciting its pleasures, charitable effects, virtues attendant upon it, and its utility to the public—Contrasted by European artificial society—Further effects of Competence on Society, particularly in improving the People at large—African appears—State of Negro Slavery in Connecticut—Effects of Slavery on the African, from his childhood through life—Slavery generally characterized—West-Indian Slavery—True cause of the calamities of the West-Indies—Church—Effects of the Sabbath—Academic School—School-master—House of Sloth—Female Worthy—Inferior Schools—Female Visit—What is not, and what is, a social female visit—Pleasure of living in an improving state of society, contrasted by the dullness of stagnated society—Emigrations to the Western Country—Conclusion.

GREENFIELD HILL.

PART II.

The FLOURISHING VILLAGE.

Fair Verna! loveliest village of the west;
Of every joy, and every charm, possefs'd;
How pleas'd amid thy varied walks I rove,
Sweet, cheerful walks of innocence, and love,
And o'er thy smiling prospects cast my eyes,   5
And see the seats of peace, and pleasure, rise,
And hear the voice of Industry resound,
And mark the smile of Competence, around!
Hail, happy village! O'er thy cheerful lawns,
With earliest beauty, spring delighted dawns;   10
The northward sun begins his vernal smile;
The spring-bird carols o'er the cressy rill:
The shower, that patters in the ruffled stream,
The ploughboy's voice, that chides the lingering team, 15
The bee, industrious, with his busy song,
The woodman's axe, the distant groves among,
The waggon, rattling down the rugged steep,
The light wind, lulling every care to sleep,
All these, with mingled music, from below,   20
Deceive intruding sorrow, as I go.

How pleas'd, fond Recollection, with a smile,
Surveys the varied round of wintery toil!
How pleas'd, amid the flowers, that scent the plain,
Recalls the vanish'd frost, and sleeted rain ;
The chilling damp, the ice-endangering street,   25
And treacherous earth that slump'd beneath the feet.

Yet even stern winter's glooms could joy inspire :
Then social circles grac'd the nutwood fire ;
The axe resounded, at the sunny door ;
The swain, industrious, trimm'd his flaxen store ;   30
Or thresh'd, with vigorous flail, the bounding wheat,
His poultry round him pilfering for their meat ;
Or slid his firewood on the creaking snow ;
Or bore his produce to the main below ;
Or o'er his rich returns exulting laugh'd ;   35
Or pledg'd the healthful orchard's sparkling draught :
While, on his board, for friends and neighbours spread,
The turkey smoak'd, his busy housewife fed ;
And Hospitality look'd smiling round,
And Leisure told his tale, with gleeful sound.   40

Then too, the rough road hid beneath the sleigh,
The distant friend despis'd a length of way,
And join'd the warm embrace, and mingling smile,
And told of all his bliss, and all his toil ;
And, many a month elaps'd, was pleas'd to view   45
How well the houshold far'd, the children grew ;
While tales of sympathy deceiv'd the hour,
And Sleep, amus'd, resign'd his wonted power.

Yes ! let the proud despise, the rich deride,
These humble joys, to Competence allied :   50
To me, they bloom, all fragrant to my heart,
Nor ask the pomp of wealth, nor gloss of art.
And as a bird, in prison long confin'd,
Springs from his open'd cage, and mounts the wind,

Thro' fields of flowers, and fragrance, gaily flies,   55
Or re-assumes his birth-right, in the skies:
Unprison'd thus from artificial joys,
Where pomp fatigues, and fusful fashion cloys,
The soul, reviving, loves to wander free
Thro' native scenes of sweet simplicity;   60
Thro' Peace', low vale, where Pleasure lingers long,
And every songster tunes his sweetest song,
And Zephyr hastes, to breathe his first perfume,
And Autumn stays, to drop his latest bloom:
'Till grown mature, and gathering strength to roam,   65
She lifts her lengthen'd wings, and seeks her home.

But now the wintery glooms are vanish'd all;
The lingering drift behind the shady wall;
The dark-brown spots, that patch'd the snowy field;
The surly frost, that every bud conceal'd;   70
The russet veil, the way with slime o'erspread,
And all the saddening scenes of March are fled.

Sweet-smiling village! loveliest of the hills!
How green thy groves! How pure thy glassy rills!
With what new joy, I walk thy verdant streets!   75
How often pause, to breathe thy gale of sweets;
To mark thy well-built walls! thy budding fields!
And every charm, that rural nature yields;
And every joy, to Competence allied,
And every good, that Virtue gains from Pride!   80

No griping landlord here alarms the door,
To halve, for rent, the poor man's little store.
No haughty owner drives the humble swain
To some far refuge from his dread domain;
Nor wastes, upon his robe of useless pride,   85
The wealth, which shivering thousands want beside;
Nor in one palace sinks a hundred cots;
Nor in one manor drowns a thousand lots;

E

Nor, on one table, fpread for death and pain,
Devours what would a village well fuftain.　　　90

O Competence, thou blefs'd by Heaven's decree,
How well exchang'd is empty pride for thee !
Oft to thy cot my feet delighted turn,
To meet thy chearful fmile, at peep of morn ;
To join thy toils, that bid the earth look gay ;　　95
To mark thy fports, that hail the eve of May ;
To fee thy ruddy children, at thy board,
And fhare thy temperate meal, and frugal hoard ;
And every joy, by winning prattlers giv'n,
And every earneft of a future Heaven.　　　100

There the poor wanderer finds a table fpread,
The firefide welcome, and the peaceful bed.
The needy neighbour, oft by wealth denied,
There finds the little aids of life fupplied ;
The horfe, that bears to mill the hard-earn'd grain ;　105
The day's work given, to reap the ripen'd plain ;
The ufeful team, to houfe the precious food,
And all the offices of real good.

There too, divine Religion is a gueft,
And all the Virtues join the daily feaft.　　　110
Kind Hofpitality attends the door,
To welcome in the ftranger and the poor ;
Sweet Chaftity, ftill blufhing as fhe goes ;
And Patience fmiling at her train of woes ;
And meek-eyed Innocence, and Truth refin'd,　　115
And Fortitude, of bold, but gentle mind.

Thou pay'ft the tax, the rich man will not pay ;
Thou feed'ft the poor, the rich man drives away.
Thy fons, for freedom, hazard limbs, and life,
While pride applauds, but fhuns the manly ftrife :　120
Thou prop'ft religion's caufe, the world around,
And fhew'ft thy faith in works, and not in found.

Say, child of paffion! while, with idiot ftare,
Thou feeft proud grandeur wheel her funny car;
While kings, and nobles, roll befpangled by,   125
And the tall palace leffens in the fky;
Say, while with pomp thy giddy brain runs round,
What joys, like thefe, in fplendour can be found?
Ah, yonder turn thy wealth-inchanted eyes,
Where that poor, friendlefs wretch expiring lies!   130
Hear his fad partner fhriek, befide his bed,
And call down curfes on her landlord's head,
Who drove, from yon fmall cot, her houfhold fweet,
To pine with want, and perifh in the ftreet.
See the pale tradefman toil, the livelong day,   135
To deck imperious lords, who never pay!
Who wafte, at dice, their boundlefs breadth of foil,
But grudge the fcanty meed of honeft toil.
See hounds and horfes riot on the ftore,
By HEAVEN created for the haplefs poor!   140
See half a realm one tyrant fcarce fuftain,
While meagre thoufands round him glean the plain!
See, for his miftrefs' robe, a village fold,
Whofe matrons fhrink from nakednefs and cold!
See too the Farmer prowl around the fhed,   145
To rob the ftarving houfhold of their bread;
And feize, with cruel fangs, the helplefs fwain,
While wives, and daughters, plead, and weep, in vain;
Or yield to infamy themfelves, to fave
Their fire from prifon, famine, and the grave.   150

There too foul luxury taints the putrid mind,
And flavery there imbrutes the reafoning kind:
There humble worth, in damps of deep defpair,
Is bound by poverty's eternal bar:
No motives bright the etherial aim impart,   155
Nor one fair ray of hope allures the heart.

But, O fweet Competence! how chang'd the fcene,
Where thy foft footfteps lightly print the green!

Where Freedom walks erect, with manly port,
And all the bleffings to his fide refort,   160
In every hamlet, Learning builds her fchools,
And beggars, children gain her arts, and rules;
And mild Simplicity o'er manners reigns,
And blamelefs morals Purity fuftains.

From thee the rich enjoyments round me fpring,   165
Where every farmer reigns a little king;
Where all to comfort, none to danger, rife;
Where pride finds few, but nature all fupplies;
Where peace and fweet civility are feen,
And meek good-neighbourhood endears the green.   170
Here every clafs (if claffes thofe we call,
Where one extended clafs embraces all,
All mingling, as the rainbow's beauty blends,
Unknown where every hue begins or ends)
Each following, each, with uninvidious ftrife,   175
Wears every feature of improving life.
Each gains from other comelinefs of drefs,
And learns, with gentle mein to win and blefs,
With welcome mild the ftranger to receive,
And with plain, pleafing decency to live.   180
Refinement hence even humbleft life improves;
Not the loofe fair, that form and frippery loves;
But fhe, whofe manfion is the gentle mind,
In thought, and action, virtuoufly refin'd.
Hence, wives and hufbands act a lovelier part,   185
More juft the conduct, and more kind the heart;
Hence brother, fifter, parent, child, and friend,
The harmony of life more fweetly blend;
Hence labour brightens every rural fcene;
Hence cheerful plenty lives along the green;   190
Still Prudence eyes her hoard, with watchful care,
And robes of thrift and neatnefs, all things wear.

But hark! what voice fo gaily fills the wind?
Of care oblivious, whofe that laughing mind?

'Tis yon poor black, who ceafes now his fong,   195
And whiftling, drives the cumbrous wain along.
He never, dragg'd, with groans, the galling chain ;
Nor hung, fufpended, on th' infernal crane ;
No dim, white fpots deform his face, or hand,
Memorials hellifh of the marking brand !   200
No feams of pincers, fcars of fcalding oil ;
No wafte of famine, and no wear of toil.
But kindly fed, and clad, and treated, he
Slides on, thro' life, with more than common glee.
For here mild manners good to all impart,   205
And ftamp with infamy th' unfeeling heart ;
Here law, from vengeful rage, the flave defends,
And here the gofpel peace on earth extends.

He toils, 'tis true ; but fhares his mafter's toil ;
With him, he feeds the herd, and trims the foil ;   210
Helps to fuftain the houfe, with clothes, and food,
And takes his portion of the common good :
Loft liberty his fole, peculiar ill,
And fix'd fubmiffion to another's will.
Ill, ah, how great ! without that cheering fun,   215
The world is chang'd to one wide, frigid zone ;
The mind, a chill'd exotic, cannot grow,
Nor leaf with vigour, nor with promife blow ;
Pale, fickly, fhrunk, it ftrives in vain to rife,
Scarce lives, while living, and untimely dies.   220

See frefh to life the Afric infant fpring,
And plume its powers, and fpread its little wing !
Firm is it's frame, and vigorous is its mind,
Too young to think, and yet to mifery blind.
But foon he fees himfelf to flavery born ;   225
Soon meets the voice of power, the eye of fcorn ;
Sighs for the bleffings of his peers, in vain ;
Condition'd as a brute, tho' form'd a man.

Around he cafts his fond, inftinctive eyes,
And fees no good, to fill his wifhes, rife :   230
(No motive warms, with animating beam,
Nor praife, nor property, nor kind efteem,
Blefs'd independence, on his native ground,
Nor fweet equality with thofe around ;)
Himfelf, and his, another's fhrinks to find,   235
Levell'd below the lot of human kind.
Thus, fhut from honour's paths, he turns to fhame,
And filches the fmall good, he cannot claim.
To four, and ftupid, finks his active mind ;
Finds joys in drink, he cannot elfewhere find ;   240
Rule difobeys ; of half his labour cheats ;
In fome fafe cot, the pilfer'd turkey eats ;
Rides hard, by night, the fteed, his art purloins ;
Serene from confcience' bar himfelf effoins ;
Sees from himfelf his fole redrefs muft flow,   245
And makes revenge the balfam of his woe.

   Thus flavery's blaft bids fenfe and virtue die ;
Thus lower'd to duft the fons of Afric lie.
Hence fages grave, to lunar fyftems given,
Shall afk, why two-legg'd brutes were made by HEAVEN; 250
HOME feek, what pair firft peopled Afric's vales,
And nice MONBODDO calculate their tails.

   O thou chief curfe, fince curfes here began ;
Firft guilt, firft woe, firft infamy of man ;
Thou fpot of hell, deep fmirch'd on human kind,   255
The uncur'd gangrene of the reafoning mind ;
Alike in church, in ftate, and houfhold all,.
Supreme memorial of the world's dread fall ;
O flavery ! laurel of the Infernal mind,
Proud Satan's triumph over loft mankind !   260

   See the fell Spirit mount his footy car !
While Hell's black trump proclaims the finifh'd war ;
Her choiceft fiends his wheels exulting draw,
And fcream the fall of GOD's moft holy law.

In dread proceffion fee the pomp begin,   265
Sad pomp of woe, of madnefs, and of fin!
Grav'd on the chariot, all earth's ages roll,
And all her climes, and realms, to either pole.
Fierce in the flafh of arms, fee Europe fpread!
Her jails, and gibbets, fleets, and hofts, difplay'd!   270
Awe-ftruck, fee filken Afia filent bow!
And feeble Afric writhe in blood below!
Before, peace, freedom, virtue, blifs, move on,
The fpoils, the treafures, of a world undone;
Behind, earth's bedlam millions clank the chain,   275
Hymn their difgrace, and celebrate their pain;
Kings, nobles, priefts, dread fenate! lead the van,
And fhout "Te-Deum!" o'er defeated man.

Oft, wing'd by thought, I feek thofe Indian ifles,
Where endlefs fpring, with endlefs fummer fmiles, 280
Where fruits of gold untir'd Vertumnus pours,
And Flora dances o'er undying flowers.
There, as I walk thro' fields, as Eden gay,
And breathe the incenfe of immortal May,
Ceafelefs I hear the fmacking whip refound;   285
Hark! that fhrill fcream! that groan of death-bed found!
See thofe throng'd wretches pant along the plain,
Tug the hard hoe, and figh in hopelefs pain!
Yon mother, loaded with her fucking child,
Her rags with frequent fpots of blood defil'd,   290
Drags flowly fainting on; the fiend is nigh;
Rings the fhrill cowfkin; roars the tyger-cry;
In pangs, th' unfriended fuppliant crawls along,
And fhrieks the prayer of agonizing wrong.

Why glows yon oven with a fevenfold fire?   295
Crifp'd in the flames, behold a man expire!
Lo! by that vampyre's hand, yon infant dies,
It's brains dafh'd out, beneath it's father's eyes.

(40)

Why fhrinks yon flave, with horror, from his meat?
Heavens! 'tis his flefh, the wretch is whipp'd to eat. 300
Why ftreams the life-blood from that female's throat?
She fprinkled gravy on a gueft's new coat!

.   .   .   .   .   .   ,

.   .   .   .   .

Why croud thofe quivering blacks yon dock around? 305
Thofe fcreams announce; that cowfkin's fhrilling found.
See, that poor victim hanging from the crane,
While loaded weights his limbs to torture ftrain;
At each keen ftroke, far fpouts the burfting gore,
And fhrieks, and dying groans, fill all the fhore. 310
Around, in throngs, his brother-victims wait,
And feel, in every ftroke, their coming fate;
While each, with palfied hands, and fhuddering fears,
The caufe, the rule, and price, of torment bears.

Hark, hark, from morn to night, the realm around, 315
The cracking whip, keen taunt, and fhriek, refound!
O'ercaft are all the fplendors of the fpring;
Sweets court in vain; in vain the warblers fing;
Illufions all! 'tis Tartarus round me fpreads
His difmal fcreams, and melancholy fhades. 320
The damned, fure, here clank th' eternal chain,
And wafte with grief, or agonize with pain.
A Tartarus new! inverfion ftrange of hell!
Guilt wreaks the vengeance, and the guiltlefs feel.
The heart, not form'd of flint, here all things rend; 325
Each fair a fury, and each man a fiend;
From childhood, train'd to every baleful ill,
And their firft fport, to torture, and to kill.

Afk not, why earthquakes rock that fateful land;
Fires wafte the city; ocean whelms the ftrand; 330
Why the fierce whirlwind, with electric fway,
Springs from the ftorm, and faftens on his prey,

Shakes heaven, rends earth, upheaves the cumbrous wave,
And with destruction's besom fills the grave:
Why dark disease roams swift her nightly round,   335
Knocks at each door, and wakes the gasping sound.

Ask, shuddering ask, why, earth-embosom'd sleep
The unbroken fountains of the angry deep :
Why, bound, and furnac'd, by the globe's strong frame,
In sullen quiet, waits the final flame :   340
Why surge not, o'er yon isles it's spouting fires,
'Till all their living world in dust expires.
Crimes found their ruin's moral cause aloud,
And all heaven, sighing, rings with cries of brother's blood.

Beside yon church, that beams a modest ray,   345
With tidy neatness reputably gay,
When, mild and fair, as Eden's seventh-day light,
In silver silence, shines the Sabbath bright,
In neat attire, the village housholds come,
And learn the path-way to the eternal home.   350
Hail solemn ordinance ! worthy of the Skies ;
Whence thousand richest blessings daily rise ;
Peace, order, cleanliness, and manners sweet,
A sober mind, to rule submission meet,
Enlarging knowledge, life from guilt refin'd,   355
And love to God, and friendship to mankind.
In the clear splendour of thy vernal morn,
New-quicken'd man to light, and life, is born ;
The desert of the mind with virtue blooms ;
It's flowers unfold, it's fruits exhale perfumes ;   360
Proud guilt dissolves, beneath the searching ray,
And low debasement, trembling, creeps away ;
Vice bites the dust ; foul Error seeks her den ;
And God, descending, dwells anew with men.
Where yonder humbler spire salutes the eye,   365
It's vane slow turning in the liquid sky,

F

Where, in light gambols, healthy ftriplings fport,
Ambitious learning builds her outer court;
A grave preceptor, there, her ufher ftands,
And rules, without a rod, her little bands.	370
Some half-grown fprigs of learning grac'd his brow:
Little he knew, though much he wifh'd to know,
Inchanted hung o'er Virgil's honey'd lay,
And fmil'd, to fee defipient Horace play;
Glean'd fcraps of Greek; and, curious, trac'd afar,	375
Through Pope's clear glafs, the bright Mæonian ftar.
Yet oft his ftudents at his wifdom ftar'd,
For many a ftudent to his fide repair'd,
Surpriz'd, they heard him Dilworth's knots untie,
And tell, what lands beyond the Atlantic lie.	380

Many his faults; his virtues fmall, and few;
Some little good he did, or ftrove to do;
Laborious ftill, he taught the early mind,
And urg'd to manners meek, and thoughts refin'd;
Truth he imprefs'd, and every virtue prais'd;	385
While infant eyes, in wondering filence, gaz'd;
The worth of time would, day by day, unfold,
And tell them, every hour was made of gold.
Brown Induftry he lov'd; and oft declar'd
How hardy Sloth, in life's fad evening, far'd;	390
Through grave examples, with fage meaning, ran,
Whilft was each form, and thus the tale began.

" Befide yon lonely tree, whofe branches bare
Rife white, and murmur to the paffing air,
There, where the twining briars the yard enclofe,	395
The houfe of Sloth ftands hufh'd in long repofe."

" In a late round of folitary care,
My feet inftinct to rove, they knew not where,
I thither came. With yellow bloffoms gay,
The tall rank weed begirt the tangled way:	400

Curious to view, I forc'd a path between,
And climb'd the broken ftile, and gaz'd the fcene."

" O'er an old well, the curb half-fallen fpread,
Whofe boards, end-loofe, a mournful creaking made;
Poiz'd on a leaning poft, and ill-fuftain'd,   405
In ruin fad, a mouldering fwepe remain'd;
Ufelefs, the crooked pole ftill dangling hung,
And, tied with thrumbs, a broken bucket fwung."

" A half-made wall around the garden lay,
Mended, in gaps, with brufhwood in decay.   410
No culture through the woven briars was feen,
Save a few fickly plants of faded green :
The ftarv'd potatoe hung it's blafted feeds,
And fennel ftruggled to o'ertop the weeds.
There gaz'd a ragged fheep, with wild furprife,   415
And too lean geefe upturn'd their flanting eyes."

" The cottage gap'd, with many a difmal yawn,
Where, rent to burn, the covering boards were gone;
Or, by one nail, where others endwife hung,
The fky look'd thro', and winds portentous rung.   420
In waves, the yielding roof appear'd to run,
And half the chimney-top was fallen down."

" The ancient cellar-door, of ftructure rude,
With tatter'd garments calk'd, half open ftood.
There, as I peep'd, I faw the ruin'd bin;   425
The fills were broke; the wall had crumbled in;
A few, long-emptied cafks lay mouldering round,
And wafted afhes fprinkled o'er the ground;
While, a fad fharer in the houfhold ill,
A half-ftarv'd rat crawl'd out, and bade farewell."   430

" One window dim, a loop-hole to the fight,
Shed round the room a pale, penurious light;

Here rags gay-colour'd eked the broken glafs;
There panes of wood fupplied the vacant fpace."

" As, pondering deep, I gaz'd, with gritty roar,   435
The hinges creak'd, and open ftood the door.
Two little boys, half-naked from the waift,
With ftaring wonder, ey'd me, as I pafs'd.
The fmile of Pity blended with her tear—
Ah me! how rarely Comfort vifits here!"   440

" On a lean hammoc, once with feathers fill'd,
His limbs by dirty tatters ill conceal'd,
Tho' now the fun had rounded half the day,
Stretch'd at full length, the lounger fnoring lay:
While his fad wife, befide her dreffer ftood,   445
And wafh'd her hungry houfhold's meagre food,
His aged fire, whofe beard, and flowing hair,
Wav'd filvery, o'er his antiquated chair,
Rofe from his feat; and, as he watch'd my eye,
Deep from his bofom heav'd a mournful figh—   450
" Stranger, he cried, once better days I knew;"
And, trembling, fhed the venerable dew.
I wifh'd a kind reply; but wifh'd in vain;
No words came timely to relieve my pain:
To the poor parent, and her infants dear,   455
Two mites I gave, befprinkled with a tear;
And, fix'd again to fee the wretched fhed,
Withdrew in filence, clos'd the door, and fled."

" Yet this fo lazy man I've often feen
Hurrying, and buftling, round the bufy green;   460
The loudeft prater, in a blackfmith's fhop;
The wifeft ftatefman, o'er a drunken cup;
(His fharp-bon'd horfe, the ftreet that nightly fed,
Tied, many an hour, in yonder tavern-fhed)
In every gambling, racing match, abroad: 465
But a rare hearer, in the houfe of God."

" Such, fuch, my children, is the difmal cot,
Where drowfy Sloth receives her wretched lot :
But O how different is the charming cell,
Where Induftry and Virtue love to dwell !"   470

" Beyond that hillock, topp'd with fcatter'd trees,
That meet, with frefheft green, the haftening breeze,
There, where the glaffy brook reflects the day,
Nor weeds, nor fedges, choke its cryftal way,
Where budding willows feel the earlieft fpring,   475
And wonted red-breafts fafely neft, and fing,
A female Worthy lives ; and all the poor
Can point the way to her fequefter'd door."

" She, unfeduc'd by drefs and idle fhew,
The forms, and rules, of fafhion never knew ;   480
Nor glittering in the ball, her form difplay'd ;
Nor yet can tell a diamond, from a fpade.
Far other objects claim'd her fteady care ;
The morning chapter, and the nightly prayer ;
The frequent vifit to the poor man's fhed ;   485
The wakeful nurfing, at the fick man's bed ;
Each day, to rife, before the early fun ;
Each day, to fee her daily duty done ;
To cheer the partner of her houfhold cares,
And mould her children, from their earlieft years.   490

" Small is her houfe ; but fill'd with ftores of good ;
Good, earn'd with toil, and with delight beftow'd.
In the clean cellar, rang'd in order neat,
Gay-fmiling Plenty boafts her cafks of meat,
Points, to fmall eyes, the bins where apples glow,   495
And marks her cyder-butts, in ftately row.
Her granary, fill'd with harveft's various pride,
Still fees the poor man's bufhel laid afide ;
Here fwells the flaxen, there the fleecy ftore,
And the long wood-pile mocks the winter's power :   500

White are the fwine; the poultry plump and large;
For every creature thrives, beneath her charge."

" Plenteous, and plain, the furniture is feen;
All form'd for ufe, and all as filver clean.
On the clean dreffer, pewter fhines arow;　　　　505
The clean-fcower'd bowls are trimly fet below;
While the wafh'd coverlet, and linen white,
Affure the traveller a refrefhing night."

" Oft have I feen, and oft ftill hope to fee,
This friend, this parent to the poor and me,　　　510
Tho' bent with years, and toil, and care, and woe,
Age lightly filver'd on her furrow'd brow,
Her frame ftill ufeful, and her mind ftill young,
Her judgment vigorous, and her memory ftrong,
Serene her fpirits, and her temper fweet,　　　　515
And pleas'd the youthful circle ftill to meet,
Cheerful, the long-accuftom'd tafk purfue,
Prevent the ruft of age, and life renew;
To church, ftill pleas'd, and able ftill, to come,
And fhame the lounging youth, who fleep at home."　520

" Such as her toils, has been the bright reward;
For Heaven will always toils like thefe regard.
Safe, on her love, her truth and wifdom tried,
Her hufband's heart, thro' lengthened life, relied;
From little, daily faw his wealth increafe,　　　525
His neighbours love him, and his houfhold blefs;
In peace and plenty liv'd, and died refign'd,
And, dying, left fix thoufand pounds behind.
Her children, train'd to ufefulnefs alone,
Still love the hand, which led them kindly on,　　530
With pious duty, own her wife beheft,
And, every day, rife up, and call her blefs'd."

" More would ye know, of each poor hind enquire,
Who fees no fun go down upon his hire;

A cheerful witnefs, bid each neighbour come ; 535
Afk each fad wanderer, where he finds a home ;
His tribute even the vileft wretch will give,
And praife the ufeful life, he will not live."

" Oft have the prattlers, GOD to me has giv'n,
The flock, I hope, and ftrive, to train for Heaven, 540
With little footfteps, fought her manfion dear,
To meet the welcome, given with heart fincere ;
And cheer'd with all, that early minds can move,
The fmiles of gentlenefs, and acts of love,
At home, in lifping tales, her worth difplay'd, 545
And pour'd their infant bleffings on her head."

" Ye kings, of pomp, ye nobles proud of blood,
Heroes of arms, of fcience fages proud !
Read, blufh, and weep, to fee, with all your ftore,
Fame, genius, knowledge, bravery, wealth, and power, 550
Crown'd, laurell'd, worfhipp'd, gods beneath the fun,
Far lefs of real good enjoy'd, or done."

Such leffons, pleas'd, he taught. The precepts new
Oft the young train to early wifdom drew ;
And, when his influence willing minds confefs'd, 555
The children lov'd him, and the parents blefs'd ;
But, when by foft indulgence led aftray,
His pupil's hearts had learn'd the idle way,
Tho' conftant, kind, and hard, his toils had been,
For all thofe toils, fmall thanks had he, I ween. 560

Behold yon humbler manfion lift its head !
Where infant minds to fcience door are led.
As now, by kind indulgence loofs'd to play,
From place to place, from fport to fport, they ftray,
How light their gambols frolic o'er the green ! 565
How their fhrill voices cheer the rural fcene !
Sweet harmlefs elves ! in Freedom's houfhold born,
Enjoy the raptures of your tranfient morn ;

And let no hour of anxious manhood see
Your minds lefs innocent, or blefs'd, or free!   570
　　See too, in every hamlet, round me rife
A central fchool-houfe, drefs'd in modeft guife!
Where every child for ufeful life prepares,
To bufinefs moulded, ere he knows its cares;
In worth matures, to independence grows,   575
And twines the civic garland o'er his brows.

　　Mark, how invited by the vernal fky,
Yon cheerful group of females paffes by!
Whofe hearts, attun'd to focial joy, prepare
A friendly vifit to fome neighbouring fair.   580
How neatnefs gliftens from the lovely train!
Bright charm! which pomp to rival tries in vain.

　　Ye Mufes! dames of dignified renown,
Rever'd alike in country, and in town,
Your bard the myfteries of a vifit fhow;   585
For fure your Ladyfhips thofe myfteries know:
What is it then, obliging Sifters! fay,
The debt of focial vifiting to pay?

　　'Tis not to toil before the idol pier;
To fhine the firft in fafhion's lunar fphere;   590
By fad engagements forc'd, abroad to roam,
And dread to find the expecting fair, at home!
To ftop at thirty doors, in half a day,
Drop the gilt card, and proudly roll away;
To alight, and yield the hand, with nice parade;   595
Up ftairs to ruftle in the ftiff brocade;
Swim thro' the drawing room, with ftudied air;
Catch the pink'd beau, and fhade the rival fair;
To fit, to curb, to tofs, with bridled mien,
Mince the fcant fpeech, and lofe a glance between;   600
Unfurl the fan, difplay the fnowy arm,
And ope, with each new motion, fome new charm:

Or fit, in filent folitude, to fpy
Each little failing, with malignant eye;
Or chatter, with inceffancy of tongue,   605
Carelefs, if kind, or cruel, right, or wrong;
To trill of us, and ours, of mine, and me,
Our houfe, our coach, our friends, our family,
While all th' excluded circle fit in pain,
And glance their cool contempt, or keen difdain: 610
T' inhale, from proud Nanking, a fip of tea,
And wave a curtfey trim, and flirt away:
Or wafte, at cards, peace, temper, health and life,
Begin with fullennefs, and end in ftrife,
Lofe the rich feaft, by friendly converfe given, 615
And backward turn from happinefs, and heaven.

It is, in decent habit, plain and neat,
To fpend a few choice hours, in converfe fweet;
Carelefs of forms, to act th' unftudied part,
To mix in friendfhip, and to blend the heart; 620
To choofe thofe happy themes, which all muft feel,
The moral duties, and the houfhold weal,
The tale of fympathy, the kind defign,
Where rich affections foften, and refine;
T' amufe, to be amus'd, to blefs, be blefs'd, 625
And tune to harmony the common breaft;
To cheer, with mild good-humour's fprightly ray,
And fmooth life's paffage, o'er its thorny way;
To circle round the hofpitable board,
And tafte each good, our generous climes afford; 630
To court a quick return, with accents kind,
And leave, at parting, fome regret behind.

Such, here, the focial intercourfe is found;
So flides the year, in fmooth enjoyment, round.

Thrice blefs'd the life, in this glad region fpent, 635
In peace, in competence, and ftill content;

G

Where bright, and brighter, all things daily fmile,
And rare and fcanty, flow the ftreams of ill;
Where undecaying youth fits blooming round,
And Spring looks lovely on the happy ground;   640
Improvement glows, along life's cheerful way,
And with foft luftre makes the paffage gay.
Thus oft, on yonder Sound, when evening gales
Breath'd e'or th' expanfe, and gently fill'd the fails,
The world was ftill, the heavens were drefs'd in fmiles, 645
And the clear moon-beam tipp'd the diftant ifles,
On the blue plain a lucid image gave,
And capp'd, with filver light, each little wave;
The filent fplendour, floating at our fide,
Mov'd as we mov'd, and wanton'd on the tide;   650
While fhadowy points, and havens, met the eye,
And the faint-glimmering landmark told us home was nigh.

Ah, dire reverfe! in yonder eaftern clime,
Where heavy drags the fluggifh car of time;
The world unalter'd by the change of years,   655
Age after age, the fame dull afpect wears;
On the bold mind the weight of fyftem fpread,
Refiftlefs lies, a cumbrous load of lead;
One beaten courfe, the wheels politic keep,
And flaves of cuftom, lofe their woes in fleep;   660
Stagnant is focial life; no bright defign,
Quickens the floth, or checks the fad decline.
The friend of man cafts round a wifhful eye,
And hopes, in vain, improving fcenes to fpy;
Slow o'er his head, the dragging moments roll,   665
And damp each cheerful purpofe of the foul.

Thus the bewilder'd traveller, forc'd to roam
Through a lone foreft, leaves his friends, and home;
Dun evening hangs the fky; the woods around
Join their dun umbrage o'er the ruffet ground;   670
At every ftep, new gloom infhrouds the fkies;
His path grows doubtful, and his fears arife:

No woodland fongftrefs foothes his mournful way ;
No taper gilds the gloom with cheering ray ;
On the cold earth he laps his head forlorn,   675
And watching, looks, and looks, to fpy the lingering morn.

And when new regions prompt their feet to roam,
And fix, in untrod fields, another home,
No dreary realms our happy race explore,
Nor mourn their exile from their native fhore.   680
For there no endlefs frofts the glebe deform,
Nor blows, with icy breath, perpetual ftorm :
No wrathful funs, with fickly fplendour glare,
Nor moors, impoifon'd, taint the balmy air,
But medial climates change the healthful year ;   685
Pure ftreamlets wind, and gales of Eden cheer ;
In mifty pomp the fky-topp'd mountains ftand,
And with green bofom humbler hills expand :
With flowery brilliance fmiles the woodland glade ;
Full teems the foil, and fragrant twines the fhade.   690
There cheaper fields the numerous houfhold charm,
And the glad fire gives every fon a farm ;
In falling forefts, Labour's axe refounds ;
Opes the new field ; and wind the fence's bounds ;
The green wheat fparkles ; nods the towering corn ;   695
And meads, and paftures, leffening waftes adorn.
Where howl'd the foreft, herds unnumber'd low ;
The fleecy wanderers fear no prowling foe ;
The village fprings ; the humble fchool afpires ;
And the church brightens in the morning fires !   700
Young Freedom wantons ; Art exalts her head ;
And infant Science prattles through the fhade.
There changing neighbours learn their manners mild ;
And toil and prudence drefs th' improving wild :
The favage fhrinks, nor dares the blifs annoy ;   705.
And the glad traveller wonders at the joy.

All hail, thou weſtern world! by heaven deſign'd
Th' example bright, to renovate mankind.
Soon ſhall thy ſons acroſs the mainland roam;
And claim, on far Pacific ſhores, their home;   710
Their rule, religion, manners, arts, convey,
And ſpread their freedom to the Aſian ſea.
Where erſt ſix thouſand ſuns have roll'd the year
O'er plains of ſlaughter, and o'er wilds of fear,
Towns, cities, fanes, ſhall lift their towery pride;   715
The village bloom, on every ſtreamlets ſide;
Proud Commerce, mole the weſtern ſurges lave;
The long, white ſpire lie imag'd on the wave;
O'er morn's pellucid main expand their ſails,
And the ſtarr'd enſign court Korean gales.   720
Then nobler thoughts ſhall ſavage trains inform;
Then barbarous paſſions ceaſe the heart to ſtorm:
No more the captive circling flames devour;
Through the war path the Indian creep no more;
No midnight ſcout the ſlumbering village fire;   725
Nor the ſcalp'd infant ſtain his gaſping ſire:
But peace, and truth, illume the twilight mind,
The goſpel's ſunſhine, and the purpoſe kind.
Where marſhes teem'd with death, ſhall meads unfold;
Untrodden cliffs reſign their ſtores of gold;   730
The dance refin'd on Albion's margin move,
And her lone bowers rehearſe the tale of love.
Where ſlept perennial night, ſhall ſcience riſe,
And new-born Oxfords cheer the evening ſkies;
Miltonic ſtrains the Mexic hills prolong,   735
And Louis murmurs to Sicilian ſong.

Then to new climes the bliſs ſhall trace its way,
And Tartar deſarts hail the riſing day;
From the long torpor ſtartled China wake;
Her chains of miſery rous'd Peruvia break;   740

Man link to man; with bofom bofom twine;
And one great bond the houfe of Adam join:
The facred promife full completion know,
And peace, and piety, the world o'erflow.

END OF THE SECOND PART.

GREENFIELD HILL:

A

POEM.

THE ARGUMENT.

*I*N *the beginning of July* 1779, *the British, under the command of Sir George Collyer, and Governor Tryon, plundered New-Haven. Thence they sailed to Fairfield, plundered, and burned it. Eighty-five dwelling houses, two churches, a handsome court house, several school houses, together with a great number of barns, out-houses, &c. were consumed by the fire. Many other houses were set on fire; but were extinguished by the returning inhabitants. The distress, occasioned by this act of wanton barbarity, is inconceivable; and the name of Governor Tryon will, on account of it, be remembered with the most finished detestation.*

From l. 1, *to l.* 283, *the story is related. The reader is then addressed with a representation of the happiness destroyed at Fairfield, and with an account of the prevalence of war, in ancient, and in modern times; its nature and its effects on the morals and happiness of mankind. This address extends to l,* 547, *and is succeeded by an Address to the Hero, returning victorious from war. He is first presented with a picture of the miseries of war, on the land; and is then conducted to the shore, to take a survey of maritime war.—Death—Speech of Death—Motives to abstain from war—and Conclusion.*

GREENFIELD HILL.

PART III

THE BURNING OF FAIRFIELD.

ON yon bright plain, with beauty gay,
Where waters wind, and cattle play,
Where gardens, groves, and orchards bloom,
Unconfcious of her coming doom,
Once Fairfield fmil'd. The tidy dome,   5
Of pleafure, and of peace, the home,
There rofe; and there the glittering fpire,
Secure from facrilegious fire.

And now no fcenes had brighter fmil'd,
No fkies, with purer fplendor mild,   10
No greener wreathe had crown'd the fpring,
Nor fweeter breezes fpread the wing,
Nor ftreams thro' gayer margins roll'd,
Nor harvefts wav'd with richer gold,
Nor flocks on brighter hillocks play'd,   15
Nor groves entwin'd a fafer fhade:
But o'er her plains, infernal War
Has whirl'd the terrors of his car,

H

The vengeance pour'd of wafting flame,
And blacken'd man with endlefs fhame,   20

 Long had the Briton, round our coaft,
His bolts in every haven tofs'd,
Unceafing fpread the trump's alarms,
And call'd the fwains to daily arms.
Succefs his wilder'd eye had charm'd,   25
And hope with ftrong pulfations warm'd,
And.pride, with eagle pinion, borne
Far in the blaze of fplendid morn.
With brighteft beams, as rainbows rife
To funs, departing from the fkies,   30
As morn, in April's faireft form,
Is quench'd, and buried, in the ftorm;
So brighter all his profpects fpread,
Juft as the gay enchantment fled.
His efforts clos'd in fhame forlorn;   35
His pride provok'd the taunt of fcorn;
Sunbright, the tranfient meteor fhone,
And darker left the world, when gone.

 Soft rofe the fummer's mildeft morn;
To yonder beach his fleet was borne;   40
His canvas fwell'd, his flag, unfurl'd,
Hung ruin o'er the weftern world.
Then forth his thickening thoufands came;
Their armour pour'd an eager flame,
Confufion fill'd the realm around;   45
The reaper left his fheaf unbound;
The farmer, flying, dropp'd his goad,
His oxen yok'd before the load;
His plough the unfinifh'd furrow held,
And flocks unguided roam'd the field.   50
Forth from his fhop the tradefman flew,
His mufket feizing, to purfue;
From every houfe, the hurried fwains,
Tumultuous, throng'd the buft'ling plains;

At race, the croffing fteeds were feen,   55
And crouds ftood cluftering on the green.

Aghaft the wretched townfmen fled;
The youth with nimble vigour fped ;
The virgin, wild with throbbing woe,
Flew fwift, and fwifter, from the foe ;   60
Pale Age flow totter'd on behind,
His white hair ftreaming in the wind ;
The boy, with little footfteps, hied,
And hung upon his grandfire's fide.
Clafp'd clofe, and cherifh'd at her breaft,   65
Her new-born babe the mother prefs'd ;
Oft toward the town was glanc'd her eye,
And oft fhe liften'd to the cry—
" Hafte, hafte, my babes ! the foe draws near ;
Fly, left he flay my children here"—   70
Around, the affrighted charmers fcower'd,
And fcream'd, as fierce the cannons roar'd.

The pair, beyond expreffion lov'd,
Apart, with lingering anguifh, mov'd :
He toward the war relu&ctant drew ;   75
She wav'd the long and laft adieu.

Through every field, and copfe, aftray,
The unfriended mourners trac'd their way,
That refuge in the wafte to find,
Denied them by the human kind :   80
While waggons bore, behind the throng,
The tythe of furniture along.

Meantime, in comba s ridgy van,
Dark-lowering, man confronted man ;
Tempeftuous, hoft with hoft engag'd ;   85
The fhout of thundering onfet rag'd ;
The cannon burft ; the mufquet roar'd ;
Long, fmoky folds through ether pour'd ;

Loud rofe the uproar wild ; around,
The world all trembled, at the found :   90
Now hollow groan'd the victim's cries,
And now fhrill victory fill'd the fkies.

˙*But ah ! the rude Columbian hoft
Nor leaders, arms, nor fkill, could boaft ;
To war untrain'd, they feebly bore   95
The phalanx firm of veteran power,
Scatter'd to neighbouring hills away,
And gave the fcarce-difputed day.

Yet, though in battle's rage untaught,
Superior fouls undaunted fought,   100
Atchiev'd, with breaft of generous mould,
Such deeds, as Grecian bards have told,
The patriot prov'd, the laurel gain'd,
The brave avengers of their land.

The work of crimfon flaughter done,   105
A fullen interval came on.
The fwains, efcap'd from threat'ning ill,
Hung, gloomy, round each neighbouring hill :
From houfe to houfe th' invaders flew,
To wafte, to plunder, and purfue.   110
Whatee'r their ruffian ftrength could bear
Ufeful, or pleafant, rich, or rare,
From the poor earner's feeble hand
They fnatch'd, and hurried to the ftrand.

To bruife the head of filver hair,   115
To agonize the imploring fair,
The hufband's breaft convulfe with woe,
The wife to wound with every throe,
The feeble crufh, the humble beat,
And fpurn pale Anguifh from their feet,   120
With grofs affault to tear the heart,
And fmile, and revel, o'er the fmart,

To hifs the groan, to mock the prayer,
Alike their tranfport, and their care.

There Delicacy look'd, to meet   125
Compaffion, at Neronian feet;
Compaffion, puff'd in many a fong,
And prov'd by impudence of tongue;
But found, deceiv'd by Britifh breath,
To hope was woe, to truft was death.   130

Yet let not Indignation rude
Commix the worthlefs with the good:
Sweet Candour fings, with voice benign,
And fmiles to pen the generous line,
Bright fouls there were, who felt for woe,   135
And own'd the merit of a foe;
Bright Britifh fouls, with virtue warm'd,
To reafon, and to kindnefs, charm'd,
Who footh'd the wretch with tendereft care,
Their leaders fpurn'd, and curs'd the war,   140
The forrows wept of life's fhort fpan,
And felt the kindred ties of man.

Yet thefe, even thefe (let Pity's tale
Their errors, while it tells, bewail)
Thought facred Duty's ftern commands   145
Compell'd to ill their ftruggling hands.
Fond man! can Duty bid thee do
What thou muft mourn, and others rue?
Are crimes a debt by Virtue paid?
Is GOD, where confcience fhrinks, obey'd?   150
GOD, who from every ill reftrains,
Tho' greateft good the guilt obtains;
Who, on the world's funereal day,
Will truth's divine award difplay,
Bid heaven, and earth, his vengeance fee,   155
And judge thy guilty lord, and thee?

Meantime, on yonder hills, forlorn,
The townfmen ftood, with anguifh torne,
Anguifh for thofe, they left behind,
To fears, and ills, and foes, confign'd;   160
The hufband, for his darling mate;
The father, for his children's fate;
While prefcience wrung with keeneft throe,
And faft enhanc'd fufpended woe.
When lo! dark-rolling thro' the fkies,   165
Unnumber'd fmokes began to rife:
His manfion, long to each endear'd,
Where peace, and joy, alone appear'd,
Where all the charities of life,
Of parents, children, hufband, wife,   170
With fofter, tendereft bofoms ftrove,
For garlands, in the ftrife of love;
The morn with brighter beauty drefs'd;
The evening gladden'd in the weft;
Bade each gay fun more gaily roll,   175
And twin'd the fympathy of foul;
That manfion, malice' feven-fold ire
Now wrapp'd in fwathes of circling fire,
Scatter'd his darling blifs in air,
And plung'd his heart in deep defpair.   180
O vileft of the crimes of War,
Fell partner of his bloody car,
Dread ill, to guilty mortals given,
To mark the wrath of injur'd HEAVEN;
O Conflagration! curfe intire;   185
The impoifon'd fting of baffled ire;
Of kings, of chiefs, th' immortal fhame;
The rafure of the reafoning name!
From thee, no aid the victor gains;
Nor wealth, nor ftrength, rewards his pains: 190
The fear, he fondly hopes imprefs'd,
Is chang'd to rage, in every breaft:

The victim, maddening with his woe,
With vengeance burns, a deadlier foe.
'Tis thine, to glean the waftes of war,   195
The landfchape of HEAVEN's good to mar,
Life's lateft refuge to confume,
And make the world a general tomb.

Say, Mufe indignant! whofe the hand
That hurl'd the conflagrative brand ?   200
A foe to human feelings born,
And of each future age the fcorn,
TRYON atchiev'd the deed malign,
TRYON, the name of every fin.
Hell's bafeft fiends the flame furvey'd,   205
And fmil'd, to fee deftruction fpread;
While Satan, blufhing deep, look'd on,
And Infamy difown'd her fon.

Now Night, of all her ftars forlorn,
Majeftic, up the fky was borne.   210
A cloud immenfe her mifty car,
Slow-fliding thro' the burden'd air;
Her wreathe of yew ; a cyprefs wand
Uplifted by her magic hand ;
Pale, fhrouded fears her awful train,   215
And fpectres gliding on the plain :
While Horror, o'er the fable world,
His enfigns, thro' the expanfe, unfurl'd.
When lo ! the fouthern fkies around,
Expanded wide, with turrets crown'd,   220
With umber'd fkirts, with wary gleam,
Uprofe an awful ridge of flame,
Shed far it's dreary luftre round,
And dimly ftreak'd the twilight ground.
Dark clouds, with many a difmal ftain,   225
Hung hov'ring o'er the gleamy main ;
While deep, the diftant, hollow roar
Wav'd, echoing from the illumin'd fhore ;

And, from each heaven-directed fpire,
Climb'd bending pyramids of fire.   230

   Meantime, a ftorm, in weftern fkies,
Thick, heavy, vaft, began to rife,
Roll'd fwift, on burden'd winds, along,
And brooded o'er the plundering throng,
In deeper night the heavens array'd   235
And ftretch'd it's pall of boundlefs fhade.
Forth fhot the fierce and lurid flame,
(The world dim-rifing in the beam)
Leffen'd the conflagrative fpires,
And blended, with their light, it's fires.   240
Again new darknefs fpread the main,
The fplendors bright'ning rofe again.
The thunder, with earth-rending found,
Shook every vale, and hill around;
While, at each paufe, with folemn voice,   245
The murmuring flames prolong'd the noife.
It feem'd, the final day was come,
The day of earth's protracted doom;
The Archangel's voice began to call
The nations of this guilty ball;   250
The hills to cleave; the fkies to rend;
Tumultuous elements to blend;
And HEAVEN, in pomp tremendous, came
To light the laft, funereal flame.

   The tumult pafs'd, the morn's meek eye   255
Look'd foft, and filent, from the fky.
Still on their hills the townfmen ftood,
And mark'd the fcene of ftrife, and blood,
Watching the progrefs of the day,
That bore their plundering foes away   260
Tumultuous, to the darkening ftrand
From vengeance fhrunk the guilty band,
With loads of fpoil, retir'd in hafte,
The fpoil of domes, and churches, ras'd;

Thence, to their ſhips, by boats convey'd,   265
Their ſails unfurl'd, their anchors weigh'd,
Awak'd the Injurer's ſullen ire,
And brooded o'er another fire.

Each to his home, the townſmen flew,
Where ſcenes of anguiſh met the view.   270
Here ſpread the ſunk, ſtill-blazing wall,
And there ſtood, nodding to its fall:
Here roſe the ſlow-declining fire,
And ſmoke, reluctant to expire;
There ſable brands lay ſcatter'd round,   275
And aſhes vile defac'd the ground.
The ſullen chimney frown'd alone;
The ſad winds breath'd a hollow groan:
His joys were fled; his hopes were gone;
His houſhold driven to haunts unknown: 280
There peaceful ſlumber'd Ruin wild,
And Horror. rear'd his head, and ſmil'd.

O thou! whoſe heart, with kind deſign,
Explores, and feels this honeſt line;
Before thee, lo! a village ſtands,   285
In miſery plung'd by hoſtile hands.
Such, ſuch is war's pernicious rage,
In every form, and clime, and age,
It ſweeps, where'er its horrors come,
All human bleſſings to the tomb.   290
Once, on this little ſpot, appear'd
Whate'er the life of man endear'd,
Peace, freedom, competence, and health,
Enduring good, and real wealth;
With Innocence, of tranquil breaſt,   295
Their faithful friend, and conſtant. gueſt;
While all the village Virtues ſmil'd,
And play'd, and ſung their field-notes wild.
The feaſt of temperate, houſhold joy,
That ſtill delights, that cannot cloy,   300

I

Went round the year.　The hufband's toil
Still bade the field and garden fmile ;
With green adorn'd the vernal day ;
Awak'd the tended flock to play ;
Bade Summer lay his golden load,　　　　　　　305
And Autumn drop his blooming good ;
Of froft, compell'd the rage to ceafe,
And charm'd the wintry ftorm to peace.
Her toils to his the wife conjoin'd,
With fweeteft unity of mind ;　　　　　　　　310
Converted, all he earn'd, to good,
The fleece to clothes, the corn to food ;
Preferv'd, with watchful eye, the hoard ;
With dainties crown'd the cheerful board ;
In every labour claim'd her fhare ;　　　　　　315
And burnifh'd joy, and gilded care ;
And, with a fweet, fupporting fmile,
Seren'd, and leffen'd, every ill.

　　Around, fuftain'd, inftructed, fway'd,
Their little flock, as lambkins, play'd,　　　　320
With ftripling fports, and fmiling ftrife,
Deceiv'd the thorny road of life ;
Clafp'd the fond heart ; the bofom charm'd ;
And Labour's icy finews warm'd ;
With bloffom'd hopes enchanted pain,　　　　325
And life's brown autumn green'd again.
The lovely fcene the parents view'd,
And daily faw their blifs renew'd,
Beheld themfelves, in theirs, revive,
And thro' fucceeding ages live.　　　　　　　330

　　Meantime, from houfe to houfe, went round
The cup, with focial pleafure crown'd ;
The blifs, good neighbourhood beftows,
Immingling joys, and foothing woes ;

The feaft, with fpicy fragrance, cheer'd ;   335
With glee the evening hour endear'd ;
Laid ficknefs on a downy bed ;
And pillow'd foft the weary head ;
Smooth'd the ftern brow of angry Strife,
And added balm to drooping life.   340

Here too, with fond, maternal hands,
The fchool embrac'd her infant bands ;
To wifdom led the early mind,
Affections foft, and actions kind ;
Prepar'd to fill the ufeful part,   345
And form'd to worth the cultur'd heart.

And here, when beam'd the fabbath's ray,
Bright earneft of immortal day,
The bell the folemn warning rung ;
The temple's doors unfolded hung :
To pay, each grateful houfhold came,   350
Its tribute to th' Unutter'd Name ;
And fent with heaven-directed eyes,
United incenfe to the fkies.

Where now, thou Child of Nature ! where   355
Is gone this humble blifs fincere ?
Lo ! guilty War has wafted all,
And Ruin, fummon'd at his call,
Has marr'd the good, th' ETERNAL yields,
And fown with falt the defert fields.   360

Such, Child of Nature ! fuch the fcene,
In every age, and clime, has been.
Since Nimrod firft the fpoil began,
Man ftill has toil'd to ruin man.
Search, fearch, and tell me, what has moft   365
The toils, and powers, of men engrofs'd ?
The nerves of fuffering Labour ftrain'd ?
Invention's richeft channels drain'd ?

Awak'd, and fir'd, the immenfe defign?
Devour'd th' incalculable mine? 370
And wing'd bold enterprife afar
Through danger, death, and ruin? War.
Peace' lowly vale neglected lies,
Unfeen, or pafs'd with glancing eyes.
The cultur'd field, the manfion fweet, 375
Where all the Loves, and Virtues meet,
The calm, the meek, the ufeful life,
The friend of man, the foe of ftrife,
The heart to kindnefs tun'd, are things
Too mean for ftatefmen, chiefs, and kings. 380
For there no twining laurels bloom,
Still verdant o'er the wintry tomb;
No cliffs ambitious tempt to rife,
And climb, and climb, to reach the fkies;
Nor fancy opes that bright abode, 385
Where man's transfigur'd to a god.

Yet *here* whate'er the earth's wide field,
Of comfort, hope, or joy, can yield,
Whate'er benignant SKIES defign'd,
To nurfe the form, or cheer the mind, 390
Our being's fcope, and ufe, and end,
The arts, and acts, that life befriend,
Whate'er adorns the reafoning name,
Or emulates an angel's fame,
The juft, the good, the humble, thrive, 395
And in *this fweet republic live.*

But thefe, too mean for kings, are feen
For all the trains of kings too mean.
For thefe no fenate gold beftows;
O'er thefe no ftatefman bends his brows; 400
No garlands bloom, proceffions glare;
Nor mobs, with idiot wonder, ftare;

No heralds blazon them to fame;
They rife, they fall, without a name.

Thro' earth's immeafurable bounds,   405
Thro' time's interminable rounds,
Each day has heard the clarion roar;
Each land been bath'd in human gore.
The Egyptian rule, the Affyrian throne,
Was rear'd of fpoils, and realms undone. 410
Greece redden'd earth around with blood,
And pour'd of woe an ocean flood;
Then pointed at herfelf the dart,
And brothers pierc'd a brother's heart.
The Perfian ruin'd half mankind: 415
The Macedonian wept, to find,
While brooding o'er the wrecks of joy,
No new world left him, to deftroy.
The ftructure mark of Rome's dread power!
Its marble bones! its cement gore!   420
Her fway the wafte of human joy;
The art to plunder, and deftroy;
A curfe to earth's extended climes;
A web of madnefs, woes, and crimes!
Her towers were built by galled hands; 425
In blood her proud Pantheon ftands;
Her triumphs fhow'd the tyger's prey;
And corpfes pav'd her Appian way.
In each tall temple's dread abode,
Pale fpectres hover'd round the god,   430
(The injur'd ghofts of countlefs lands,
Cut off from life by Roman hands)
Hung round, and claim'd the fpoils their own,
Shriek'd o'er their native realms undone,
Haunted each fhrine, with livid ftare,   435
And mingled groans with every prayer.

 Nor lefs, in modern days, when art
Has led to nobler fcenes the heart,

When fcience beams with vernal rays,
And lights to blifs ten thoufand ways,   440
The Gofpel, found in every tongue,
Has peace, and fweet falvation, fung,
The tyger charm'd to quit his prey,
And taught the wolf with lambs to play—
Still roars the trump's funereal found;   445
"To arms," the ftartled hills rebound;
War's iron car in thunder rolls,
From medial climes, to diftant poles.

Amaz'd, fee Europe, firft of all,
Proud Emprefs of this fuffering ball,   450
The fun of power, and arts refin'd,
The boaft, and beauty, of mankind,
The work of death, and plunder, fpread,
And riot on th' untimely dead!

When, borne by winds of fofteft wing,   455
Returns the life-renewing fpring,
The tempeft flies to earth's far ends,
And HEAVEN in peace and love defcends,
Shines in the fun's ferener ray,
Breathes in the balmy breath of May,   460
Diftills in earth-diffolving fhowers,
And glows in rainbow-painted flowers,
While wifdom works, while goodnefs warms,
In fky-born tints, and angel forms,
The new, the fweet, creation fprings,   465
And beauty blooms, and rapture fings :
Faft fwell the teeming feeds of food ;
The world is heap'd with boundlefs good :
In every fcene, the GODHEAD fmiles,
And man of rage, and luft, beguiles.   470
Then beats the drum its fierce alarm ;
Then millions, fir'd to madnefs, arm,

Fight, plunder, defolate, devour,
And drench the wafted world in gore.

Whofe name rolls down, from age to age ?   475
Whofe fplendours light th' Hiftoric page ?
Who wakes th' inrapt Mæonian fong ?
Who prompts the univerfal tongue ?
The world's great guardian, genius, god ?
The Man of fpoil, the Man of blood.   480
Cæfar, the butcher of mankind,
Loads with his praife each paffing wind ;
The general thief, adulterer, brute ;
His boaft to murder, wafte, pollute ;
Dread rival of Apollyon's fame ;   485
His labours, arts, and praife, the fame.
What moft the heart with vice defiles ;
Of worth difrobes ; of heaven beguiles ?
What bids in ftorms the paffions roll ;
Configns to appetite the foul ;   490
Bids Pride afcend th' ETERNAL's throne,
And claim the univerfe, her own ;
Ambition's vulture-wing expands,
Borne, hungry, keen, o'er fuffering lands ;
The wide world talon'd to his fway,   495
A field of death, and food, and prey ?
What lights, for fell Revenge, the pyre ;
Of Malice heats the quenchlefs fire ;
And lifts Affaffination's knife
Againft a friend's, or parent's, life ?   500
What ftretches Avarice' gulphy maw,
And opens wide her fhark-tooth'd jaw,
Both India's bowels to devour,
To drink the fea, and gorge the fhore ;
Calls forth, in viper paths, Difguife,   505
And points her thoufand tongues with lies ;
Bold, bronzy Fraud invefts in mail,
And clips his weights, and lops his fcale ;

For Honour's houſe digs Forgery's mine,
And guilds his green, impoiſoning coin ; 510
Breaks tyger Rapine's iron cage,
And ſends him looſe, to roam, and rage ;
Extortion rouſes, from his lair,
The cote t' o'erleap, the flock to tear,
To make the fenceleſs poor his food, 515
And eat their fleſh, and drink their blood ?
What fires, to phrenzy, Lewdneſs' veins ;
Throws on Adultery's neck the reins ;
Gives high-fed Rape at large to fly,
And makes the world a general ſtye ; 520
Peoples a realm with ſots, and ſwine,
And bids men live, to drink, and dine ;
Tempts burrow'd Atheiſm abroad,
To infuriate man, to hiſs at GOD,
To burſt each moral bond divine, 525
And nature's magic links disjoin,
The ſenſe of common good eraſe,
Th' etherial ſtamp of HEAVEN deface,
Dog gentle peace, bait generous worth,
Haunt juſtice, truth, and law, from earth, 530
And bid in hell's ſubjected fire,
Religion's ſky-built fane expire ?

What licks the final dregs of joy,
And leaves th' inverted veſſel dry ;
Makes earth, of virtue beſom'd clean, 535
The cage of every beaſt obſcene ;
A ruin'd dome, whoſe walls around
The hollow moan of death reſound ;
An Afric ſand ; a Greenland ſhore ;
Where life and comfort ſpring no more ; 540
An image dark and drear of hell ;
Where fiends, invok'd familiar dwell ;
Where loſt immortals Angels weep ;
Where curſes wake, and bleſſings ſleep ;

And GOD, the rebels forc'd t' abhor,   545
Repents his marr'd creation ? War.

   Say, Child of Nature ! does thy tear
Start, as thy pain'd eye wanders here ?
Thy cheek with manly blufhes burn ?
Thy wonted praife to curfes turn ?   550
Thy bofom wafte with cankering woe ?
And thy heart heave th' indignant throe ?

   Go then, ah go ! whate'er thy lot ;
Be thine the palace, or the cot,
To wield the rod, the yoke to bear,   555
A million, or a crown, to fhare,
The fenate's guided hand to fway,
Or bid the little flock obey,
Go, ere thy heart be chang'd to ftone,
Or ear find mufic in a groan,   560
Or gold the gates of pity bar,
Hate, curfe, oppofe, Tartarean war.
Difdain, defpife, with horror name,
And give to never-dying fhame,
The King, that thron'd for human good,   565
Configns his realm to wafte, and blood ;
Senates, that, form'd for general weal,
Sanction the dread decree to kill ;
Statefmen, to tygers chang'd by power,
That fmile, and feaft on human gore,   570
And chiefs, that havoc love to fpread,
And pluck their wreaths from fields of dead.

   But round thee gentle peace diffufe,
Her morning fmiles, and evening dews ;
Thy fons with love of peace inform ;   575
Their hearts with fweet affections warm ;
Bid them pernicious ftrife abhor,
And lifp the infant curfe on war.

K

Far round thee light the genial fire;
Thy neighbours, and thy friends, infpire :　　　580
United, lift the ardent prayer,
That God thy ruin'd race may fpare,
Wake in their hearts affections mild,
Sweet femblance of the meekly child,
Messiah's peaceful fway extend,　　　585
Bid kings, and chiefs, to virtue bend,
Protract of life the little fpan,·
And change the reafoning wolf to man.

And O thou Sage, by Learning taught,
With wifdom and with virtue fraught,　　　590
Whofe foul the breath of Heaven informs ;
Whofe heart Messiah's fpirit warms ;
Sleep, fleep no more.　For fuffering men,
Awake thy voice; aroufe thy pen ;
The caufe of peace and kindnefs plead ;　　　595
For mifery let thy bofom bleed ;
To endlefs hate and fhame confign
The tyger thron'd, the titled fwine ;
The charm of threefcore centuries break,
And bid the torpid flumberer wake ;　　　600
Burft with new found the adder's ear,
And make th' infenfate marble hear,
His intereft know, his end difcern,
And o'er his flaughter'd kindred yearn,
Feel the unmeafur'd curfe of war,　　　605
And all her crimfon fiends abhor :
Tread where th' impaffion'd faviour trode,
And earth fhall hail thee, Child of God.*

Go too, thou ardent Hero ! go,
Frefh from fields of war, and woe,　　　610

* Allufion to Mat. 5. ix.

From thy proud, triumphal car,
Glittering with the spoils of war,
While thy wheels majestic roll
Onward to th' immortal goal;
While thy arms with lightning blaze ;   615
While extatic millions gaze ;
Shouts to heaven thy triumphs wing,
And imagin'd angels sing ;
Lessening in th' immense parade,
All preceding glories fade,   620
Cæsar's changing star retires,
And eclips'd are Marlborough's fires ;
Cast around thee searching eyes,
Mark thy splendours, whence they rise !
See, on fields, with corses spread,   625
Thine exulting coursers tread !
See, thy car, with garlands proud,
Rolls thro' streams of human blood !
Blood from kindred bosoms pour'd !
Brothers by a brother gor'd !   630
Forth, from Adam's veins, the stream,
Living, ran through thee and them.

Mark ! around thy wandering eye,
Wasted fields of culture lie,
Late with plenteous harvests crown'd,   635
Now in gulphs of ruin drown'd.
There the HEAVENS their bounty shower'd ;
Seasons there their blessings pour'd ;
Health and comfort, clothes and food ;
Where is now the boundless good ?   640

See yon flames thro' ether bend !
See th' immense of smoke ascend !
Lost, asham'd, the sky retires,
And the sun withdraws his fires.

Cities there in ruin lie ,   645
Towns and villages of joy;
Temples, where, to virtue given,
Man was form'd for life, and Heaven;
Domes of pomp, and feats of blifs
Manfions fanctified to peace;   650
Cots, where harmlefs houfholds dwelt,
And each foft emotion felt;
Sportive play'd the wanton child,
And white Age look'd on, and fmil'd :
Streets, were cheerful Bufinefs reign'd,   655
Shops, where Toil his houfe fuftain'd ;
Humble wifhes fought, and found
Life, with peace and comfort crown'd.
Where are now the manfions dear ?
Scatter'd in the realms of air.   660
Where are now the happy trains?
Weltering on the bloody plains.
Ruin'd walls deface the ground ;
Silence broods the domes around ;
Ravens flutter o'er the tomb,   665
Vultures fcream, and tygers roam.

To the margin of the deep
Bid thy wheels of grandeur fweep.
See th' imperial fail, unfurl'd,
Wave triumphant o'er the world ;   670
Rows of fleeping cannon join'd ;
Streamers glorying on the wind !

Lo ! the proudly-fwelling gales,
Springing, fill the wanton fails ;
Marfhal'd in fublime array,   675
Winds the fleet its lordly way ;
Ocean greets the awful train,
And expands his glaffy plain.

See the private barks of prey,
Steal behind their creeping way ;   680
Arm'd, with piracy to fpoil
Hard-earn'd fruits of honeft toil ;
By the voice of Law let loofe,
Death and beggary to diffufe ;
With the dye of endlefs fhame   685
Blackening man's unhappy name !

Thron'd upon th' imperial ftern,
Death's unfinifh'd Form difcern !
Sooty clouds his limbs inclofe ;
Thorns his myftic crown compofe ;   690
In his hand, th' uplifted dart
Haftens to transfix the heart ;
From his fcythe, with lurid gleam,
Pale fulphureous lightnings ftream.

Hark, his hollow voice refounds,   695
O'er the world's unmeafur'd bounds !
Ocean quakes, thro' all his waves ;
Earth remurmurs, from her caves.

" Ceafe, fond man ! thy claims refign ;
Earth, with all her realms, is mine.   700
Thron'd with all-fubduing fway,
Here I bid the world obey.
Mine, thefe engines ocean brave ;
Mine, thefe crimfon ftreamers wave ;
Mine, the winds to waft them blow ;   705
Mine, the purple deep below.
O'er the fea, from fky to fky,
Mortals, wing'd by terror, fly :
Here, to fartheft eve, and morn,
Death's refiftlefs arms are borne ;   710
Floating hofts behind you pour ;
Hark ! purfuing thunders roar.

See your cities wrapp'd in fire!
See your fons, and fires, expire!
Infants, recent from the womb,   715
Virgins, matrons, croud the tomb!
Seas divided regions join:
All the watery world is mine."

" I ordain the crimfon day;
I the embattled hofts array;   720
Sound the trumpet, beat the alarm,
And the heart with vengeance arm.
I the ruddy ftandard fpread,
Pile the groaning fields with dead,
Light the whelming flame, and fweep   725
Every bleffing to the deep.

" Man, delighting to deftroy,
Hating peace, and fhunning joy,
Man, who feels his life too long,
Child of madnefs, child of wrong,   730
Man, obfequious to my will,
Loves the glorious work of ill,
Cuts off half his brother's years,
Swells my darling ftream of tears,
Bids deftruction round him flow,   735
Feafting fweet on human woe."

" Who fo great a king as I?
My pavilion is the fky;
Earth my realm, my throne the air;
Winds my courfers; clouds my car: 740
Suns but light me to my prey;
Midnight veils my fecret way:
O'er expiring worlds I ride;
Dearth and Plague, before me ftride:
Storms, my befom, fweep the wave,   745
And with thoufands fill the grave;

Chiefs and kings, my fervants, toil,
Butcher hofts, and countries fpoil :
Mortals every claim refign ;
Earth, air, ocean, all are mine."   75ɔ

Why, triumphant Hero ! why
Stares thy wild and tearlefs eye ?
Whence thy pale and fpectred brow ?
Palfied limbs ? and fighs of woe ?
Has the gloomy monarch's dart   755
Pierc'd with agony thy heart ?
Or has human mifery riven ?
Or the advancing curfe of Heaven ?

Thou haft fhorten'd life's fhort fpan;
Thou haft emptied earth, of man ?   760
Breafts unnumber'd rack'd with fears ;
Eyes unnumber'd drown'd in tears ;
Bidden countlefs trains expire ;
Countlefs cities funk in fire ;
Countlefs hearts with mourning riven ; 765
Countlefs fouls fhut out of heaven.

Art thou Atheift ? Spare the fpan,
Kinder Chance allows to man.
Shallow is his cup of blifs ;
Make not, then, the portion lefs :   770
Grudge not foes a boon fo fmall ;
Spare, oh fpare the little all !

But, if rais'd from mole to man,
Thou canft nobler objects fcan,
Lift thy curtain'd eyes abroad,   775
And difcern the prefent God ;
If Messiah's folar ray
Through thy night has pierc'd it's way,
And, fubliming fenfe to thought,
Has eternal wonders wrought ;   780

Think, oh think, the crimſon tide
Pours from thoſe, for whom he died !
He the millions bled to ſave,
Thou haſt hurried to the grave.
He compels, .with dread command,   785.
Every heart, and every hand,
Man to clothe, ſuſtain with food,
And to bleſs with every good ;
But, obdurate to his call,
Thou haſt ſlain, and robb'd of all.   790

 Think how precious is the hour,
Given, the wanderer to reſtore.
Think, the heart ſhall ever find
Pity from the ETERNAL MIND,
That has learn'd for man to glow,   795
Smile with joy, and weep with woe,
Give the weary outcaſt reſt,
Draw the barb from Sorrow's breaſt,
And (the ſole, alchymic ſtone)
Make a brother's weal it's own :   800
While th' unfeeling wretch ſhall meet
Vengeance at his MAKER's feet.

 But thy heart, with ill uncloy'd,
Woe has ſpread, and peace deſtroy'd,
HEAVEN's delightful work undone,   805
And the taſk of Hell begun.
Orphans' cries thy car purſue ;
Parents' tears thy path bedew ;
Widows' ſhrieks thy muſic drown ;
Cypreſs wreaths inveſt thy crown ;   810
Spoils in all thy ſplendours glow ;
Nurs'd with blood, thy laurels grow ;
On the bones of ſlaughter'd bands
See ! thy arch triumphal ſtands.

Lo ! in yonder, verging fkies,   795
Myriad troops of fpectres rife;
Spirits of a diftant world :
By thy arm to ruin hurl'd.
Briftling ftands their bloody hair ;
On thee gleams their angry ftare ; 800
In pale clouds approaching, fee
Every finger points at thee !
" Thou," they feebly murmuring cry,
" Thou haft drunk our cup of joy;
Ere the mortal race was run,   805
Quench'd in blood our noon-day fun ;
Halv'd the hour, by Mercy given,
To prepare for life, and heaven ;
And, with all our guilt unpaid,
Plung'd us to the untimely dead." 810

Fainting Hero ! pangs unknown
Break, and break, thy heart of ftone ;
Short, and fhorter, pants thy breath,
And thine eye-balls fwim in death ;
Death thy brow has whiten'd o'er ; 815
Thou art fallen, to rife no more.

END OF THE THIRD PART.

L

GREENFIELD HILL:

A

POEM.

THE ARGUMENT.

*THE Pequods inhabited the branches of the Thames, which empties itself into the Sound, at New London. This nation, from the first settlement of the English Colonists, regarded them with jealousy; and attempted to engage the neighbouring tribes in a combination against them. Several of those tribes were, however, more jealous of the Pequods, than of the English, and rejected their solicitations. Not discouraged by these disappointments, they resolved to attempt the destruction of the English, with the strength of their own tribes only; and cruelly assassinated Captains Stone, Norton, and Oldham, as they were trading peaceably in their neighbourhood. The English demanded the murderers; but were answered with disdain, and insult. Upon this, Captain Mason was dispatched into their country with a body of troops; and attacking one of their principal forts, destroyed it, together with a large number of their warriors. The rest of the nation fled. A large body of them came to a swamp, three miles westward of Fairfield. One of their number loitering behind the rest, was discovered by the English troops, then commanded by Captain Stoughton, of the Massachusetts; and was compelled to disclose their retreat. One hundred of them, it is said, surrendered. The rest, bravely resolving to live and die together, were attacked, and chiefly destroyed.** On this piece of History, the following part of the Poem is founded. It is introduced by reflections on the changes, wrought in the world by time. Ancient Empires. Great Britain. America. Story related, with reflections on the savages. Conclusion.*

* See Neale's Hist. N. Eng. and Morse's Geog.

GREENFIELD HILL.

PART IV.

THE DESTRUCTION OF THE PEQUODS.

AH me! while up the long, long vale of time,
Reflection wanders towards th' eternal vaft,
How ftarts the eye, at many a change fublime,
Unbofom'd dimly by the ages pafs'd!
What Maufoleums crowd the mournful wafte!   5
The tombs of empires fallen! and nations gone!
Each, once infcrib'd, in gold, with " AYE TO LAST"
Sate as a queen; proclaim'd the world her own,
And proudly cried, " By me no forrows fhall be known."

Soon fleets the funbright Form, by man ador'd.   10
Soon fell the Head of gold, to Time a prey;
The Arms, the Trunk, his cankering tooth devour'd;
And whirlwinds blew the Iron duft away.
Where dwelt imperial Timur?—far aftray,
Some lonely-mufing pilgrim now enquires: 15
And, rack'd by ftorms, and haftening to decay,
Mohammed's Mofque forefees it's final fires;
And Rome's more lordly Temple day by day expires.

As o'er proud Afian realms the traveller winds,
His manly fpirit, hufh'd by terror, falls;   20
When fome deceafed town's loft fite he finds,
Where ruin wild his pondering eye appals;
Where filence fwims along the moulder'd walls,
And broods upon departed Grandeur's tomb.
Through the lone, hollow aifles fad Echo calls,   25
At each flow ftep; deep fighs the breathing gloom,
And weeping fields, around, bewail their Emprefs' doom.

Where o'er an hundred realms, the throne uprofe,
The fcreech-owl nefts, the panther builds his home;
Sleep the dull newts, the lazy adders doze,   30
Where pomp and luxury danc'd the golden room.
Low lies in duft the fky-refembled dome;
Tall grafs around the broken column waves;
And brambles climb, and lonely thiftles bloom:
The moulder'd arch the weedy ftreamlet laves,
And low refound, beneath, unnumber'd funken graves.

Soon fleets the fun-bright Form, by man ador'd;
And foon man's dæmon chiefs from memory fade.
In mufty volume, now muft be explor'd,
Where dwelt imperial nations, long decay'd.   40
The brighteft meteors angry clouds invade;
And where the wonders glitter'd, none explain.
Where Carthage, with proud hand, the trident fway'd,
Now mud-wall'd cots fit fullen on the plain,
And wandering, fierce, and wild, fequefter'd Arabs reign. 45

In thee, O Albion! queen of nations, live
Whatever fplendours earth's wide realms have known;
In thee proud Perfia fees her pomp revive;
And Greece her arts; and Rome her lordly throne:
By every wind, thy Tyrian fleets are blown;   50
Supreme, on Fame's dread roll, thy heroes ftand;
All ocean's realms thy naval fcepter own;

Of bards, of fages, how auguft thy band!
And one rich Eden blooms around thy garden'd land.

But O how vaft thy crimes! Through heaven's great year, 55
When few centurial funs have trac'd their way;
When fouthern Europe, worn by feuds fevere;
Weak, doating, fallen, has bow'd to Ruffian fway;
And fetting Glory beam'd her farewell ray;
To waftes, perchance, thy brilliant fields fhall turn; 60
In duft, thy temples, towers, and towns decay;
The foreft howl, where London's turrets burn;
And all thy garlands deck thy fad, funereal urn.

Some land, fcarce glimmering in the light of fame,
Scepter'd with arts, and arms (if I divine) 65
Some unknown wild, fome fhore without a name,
In all thy pomp, fhall then majeftic fhine.
As filver-headed Time's flow years decline,
Not ruins only meet th' enquiring eye :
Where round yon mouldering oak vain brambles twine, 70
The filial ftem, already towering high,
Erelong fhall ftretch his arms, and nod in yonder fky.

Where late refounded the wild, woodland roar,
Now heaves the palace, now the temple fmiles;
Where frown'd the rude rock, and the defert fhore, 75
Now pleafure fports, and bufinefs want beguiles,
And Commerce wings her flight to thoufand ifles;
Culture walks forth; gay laugh the loaded fields;
And jocund Labour plays his harmlefs wiles;
Glad Science brightens; Art her manfion builds; 80
And Peace uplifts her wand, and HEAVEN his blefling yields.

O'er thefe fweet fields, fo lovely now, and gay,
Where modeft Nature finds each want fupplied,
Where home-born Happinefs delights to play,
And counts her little flock, with houfhold pride, 85
Long frown'd, from age to age, a foreft wide :

Here hung the flumbering bat; the ferpent dire
Nefted his brood, and drank th' impoifon'd tide;
Wolves peal'd, the dark, drear night, in hideous choir;
Nor fhrnuk th' unmeafur'd howl from Sol's terrific fire. 90

No charming cot imbank'd the pebbly ftream;
No manfion tower'd, nor garden teem'd with good;
No lawn expanded to the April beam;
Nor mellow harveft hung it's bending load;
Nor fcience dawn'd; nor life with beauty glow'd;   95
Nor temple whiten'd, in th' enchanting dell;
In clufters wild, the fluggifh wigwam ftood;
And, borne in fnaky paths, the Indian fell
Now aim'd the death unfeen, now fcream'd the tyger-yell.

Even now, perhaps, on human duft I tread,   100
Pondering, with folemn paufe, the wrecks of time;
Here fleeps, perchance, among the vulgar dead,
Some Chief, the lofty theme of Indian rhyme,
Who lov'd Ambition's cloudy fteep to climb,
And fmil'd, deaths, dangers, rivals, to engage;   105
Who rous'd his followers' fouls to deeds fublime,
Kindling to furnace heat vindictive rage,
And foar'd Cæfarean heights, the Phœnix of his age.

In yon fmall field, that dimly fteals from fight,
(From yon fmall field thefe meditations grow)   110
Turning the fluggifh foil, from morn to night,
The plodding hind, laborious, drives his plough,
Nor dreams, a nation fleeps, his foot below.
There, undifturbed by the roaring wave,
Releas'd from war, and far from deadly foe,   115
Lies down, in endlefs reft, a nation brave,
And trains, in tempefts born, there find a quiet grave.

Oft have I heard the tale, when matron fere
Sung to my infant ear the fong of woe;

Of maiden meek, confum'd with pining care,   120
Around whofe tomb the wild-rofe lov'd to blow :
Or told, with fwimming eyes, how, long ago,
Remorfelefs Indians, all in midnight dire,
The little, fleeping village, did o'erthrow,
Bidding the cruel flames to heaven afpire,   125
And fcalp'd the hoary head, and burn'd the babe with fire.

Then, fancy-fir'd, her memory wing'd it's flight,
To long-forgotten wars, and dread alarms,
To chiefs obfcure, but terrible in fight,
Who mock'd each foe, and laugh'd at deadlieft harms,   130
Sydneys in zeal, and Wafhingtons in arms.
By inftinct tender to the woes of man,
My heart bewildering with fweet pity's charms,
Thro' folemn fcenes, with Nature's ftep, fhe ran,
And hufh'd her audience fmall, and thus the tale began. 135

" Thro' verdant banks where Thames's branches glide,
Long held the Pequods an extenfive fway;
Bold, favage, fierce, of arms the glorious pride,
And bidding all the circling realms obey.
Jealous, they faw the tribes, beyond the fea,   140
Plant in their climes ; and towns, and cities, rife ;
Afcending caftles foreign flags difplay ;
Myfterious art new fcenes of life devife ;
And fteeds infult the plains, and cannon rend the fkies."

" They faw, and foon the ftrangers' fate decreed,   145
And foon of war difclos'd the crimfon fign ;
Firft, haplefs Stone ! they bade thy bofom bleed,
A guiltlefs offering at th' infernal fhrine :
Then, gallant Norton ! the hard fate was thine,
By ruffians butcher'd, and denied a grave :   150
Thee, generous Oldham ! next the doom malign
Arrefted ; nor could all thy courage fave ;
Forfaken, plunder'd, cleft, and buried in the wave."

M

" Soon the fad tidings reach'd the general ear;
And prudence, pity, vengeance, all infpire :   155
Invafive war their gallant friends prepare ;
And foon a noble band, with purpofe dire,
And threatening arms, the murderous fiends require :
Small was the band, but never taught to yield ;
Breafts fac'd with fteel, and fouls inftinct with fire :   160
Such fouls, from Sparta, Perfia's world repell'd,
When nations pav'd the ground, and Xerxes flew the field."

" The rifing clouds the Savage Chief defcried,
And, round the foreft, bade his heroes arm ;
To arms the painted warriors proudly hied,   165
And through furrounding nations rung the' alarm.
The nations heard ; but fmil'd, to fee the ftorm,
With ruin fraught, o'er Pequod mountains driven ;
And felt infernal joy the bofom warm,
To fee their light hang o'er the fkirts of even,   170
And·other funs arife, to gild a kinder heaven."

" Swift to the Pequod fortrefs Mafon fped,
Far in the wildering wood's impervious gloom ;
A lonely caftle, brown with twilight dread ;
Where oft th' embowel'd captive met his doom,   175
And frequent heav'd, around the hollow tomb ;
Scalps hung in rows, and whitening bones were ftrew'd ;
Where, round the broiling babe, frefh from the womb,
With howls the Powaw fill'd the dark abode,   180
And fcreams, and midnight prayers, invok'd the Evil god."

" There too, with awful rites, the hoary prieft,
Without, befide the mofs-grown altar, ftood,
His fable form in magic cincture drefs'd,
And heap'd the mingled offering to his god,
What time, with golden light, calm evening glow'd.   185
The myftic duft, the flower of filver bloom,
And fpicy herb, his hand in order ftrew'd ;

Bright rofe the curling flame ; and rich perfume
On fmoky wings upflew, or fettled round the tomb.''

" Then, o'er the circus, danc'd the maddening throng, 190
As erft the Thyas roam'd dread Nyfa round,
And ftruck, to foreft nofes, th' ecftatic fong,
While flow, beneath them, heav'd the wavy ground.
With a low, lingering groan, of dying found,
The woodland rumbled; murmur'd deep each ftream ; 195
Shrill fung the leaves ; all ether figh'd profound ;
Pale tufts of purple topp'd the filver flame,
And many-colour'd Forms on evening breezes came.''

" Thin, twilight Forms; attir'd in changing fheen
Of plumes, high-tinctur'd in the weftern ray ; 200
Bending, they peep'd the fleecy folds between,
Their wings light-ruftling in the breath of May.
Soft-hovering round the fire, in myftic play,
They fnuff'd the incenfe, wav'd in clouds afar,
Then, filent, floated toward the fetting day : 205
Eve redden'd each fine form, each mifty car ;
And through them faintly gleam'd, at times, the Weftern ftar.''

" Then (fo tradition fings), the train behind,
In plumy zones of rainbow'd beauty drefs'd,
Rode the Great Spirit, in th' obedient wind, 210
In yellow clouds flow-failing from the weft.
With dawning fmiles, the God his votaries blefs'd,
And taught where deer retir'd to ivy dell ;
What chofen chief with proud command to' inveft ;
Where crept th' approaching foe, with purpofe fell, 215
And where to wind the fcout, and war's dark ftorm difpel.''

" There, on her lover's tomb, in filence laid,
While ftill, and forrowing, fhower'd the moon's pale beam,
At times, expectant, flept the widow'd maid,
Her foul far-wandering on the fylph-wing'd dream. 220
Wafted from evening fkies, on funny ftream,

Her darling Youth with filver pinions fhone ;
With voice of mufic, tun'd to fweeteft theme,
He told of fhell-bright bowers, beyond the fun,
Where years of endlefs joy o'er Indian lovers run." 225

" But now no awful rites, nor potent fpell,
To filence charm'd the peals of coming war ;
Or told the dread recefles of the dell,
Where glowing Mafon led his bands from far :
No fpirit, buoyant on his airy car, 230
Controul'd the whirlwind of invading fight :
Deep died in blood, dun evening's falling ftar
Sent fad, o'er weftern hills, it's parting light,
And no returning morn difpers'd the long, dark night."

" On the drear walls a fudden fplendour glow'd , 235
There Mafon fhone, and there his veterans pour'd.
Anew the Hero claim'd the fiends of blood,
While anfwering ftorms of arrows round him fhower'd,
And the war-fcream the ear with anguifh gor'd.
Alone, he burft the gate : the foreft round 240
Re-echoed death ; the peal of onfet roar'd ;
In rufh'd the fquadrons ; earth in blood was drown'd ;
And gloomy fpirits fled, and corfes hid the ground."

Not long in dubious fight the hoft had ftriven,
When, kindled by the mufket's potent flame, 245
In clouds, and fire, the caftle rofe to heaven,
And gloom'd the world, with melancholy beam.
Then hoarfer groans, with deeper anguifh, came ;
And fiercer fight the keen affault repell'd :
Nor even thefe ills the favage breaft could tame ; 250
Like hell's deep caves, the hideous region yell'd,
'Till death, and fweeping fire, laid wafte the hoftile field."

" Soon the fad tale their friends furviving heard ;
And Mafon, Mafon, rung in every wind :

Quick from their rugged wilds they difappear'd,   255
Howl'd down the hills, and left the blaft behind.
Their faftening foes, by generous Stoughton join'd,
Hung o'er the rear, and every brake explor'd ;
But fuch dire terror feiz'd the favage mind,
So fwift and black a ftorm behind them lowr'd,   260
On wings of raging fear, thro' fpacious realms they fcowr'd."

(O thou, to earth the fecond bleffing given,
Of heart divine, of afpect angel-fweet,
O meek Religion ! fecond-born of Heaven,
Cloth'd with the fun, the world beneath thy feet !   265
Softer than lambs on yonder hillocks bleat,
Thy mufic charms to kindnefs favage man,
Since firft, from Calvary's height, with love replete,
Thy wondrous courfe, in funny fheen, began,
And, o'er the death-ftruck globe, thro' ftartled nations ran. 170

When pride and wrath awake the world to arms,
How heaves thy fnowy breaft with fainting throe !
While luft and rapine trumpet death's alarms,
And men 'gainft men with fiery vengeance glow.
In Europe oft, that land of war, and woe,   275
As her fad fteps the lingering mourner draws,
How flowly did thy feet entangled go,
Chain'd by vile tefts, and prifon'd round by laws ;
While bigotry and rage in blood infteep'd thy caufe !

When o'er th' Atlantic 'wild, by Angels borne,   280
Thy pilgrim barque explor'd it's weftern way,
With fpring and beauty bloom'd the wafte forlorn,
And night and chaos fhrunk from new-born day.
Dumb was the favage howl ; th' inftinctive lay
Wav'd, with ftrange warblings, thro' the woodland's bound; 285
The village fmil'd ; the temple's golden ray
Shot high to heaven ; fair culture clothed the ground ;
Art bloffom'd ; cities fprang ; and fails the ocean crown'd.

As on heaven's facred hill, of hills the queen,
At thy command, contention foul fhall ceafe,   290
Thy folar afpect, every ftorm ferene,
And fmooth the rugged wild of man to peace ;
So here thy voice (fair earneft of the blifs !)
Transform'd the favage to the meekly child.
Hell faw, with pangs, her hideous realm decreafe ;   295
Wolves play'd with lambs ; the tyger's heart grew mild ;
And on his own bright work the GODHEAD, look'd and fmil'd.

Hail Elliot ! Mayhew hail ! by HEAVEN inform'd
With that pure love, which clafps the human kind ;
To virtue's path even Indian feet you charm'd,   300
And lit, with wifdom's beam, the dufky mind :
From torture, blood, and treachery, refin'd,
The new-born convert lifp'd MESSIAH's name.
Mid Choirs complacent, in pure rapture join'd,
Your praife refounds, on yonder ftarry frame,   305
While fouls, redeem'd from death, their earthly faviours claim.

Oh had the fame bright fpirit ever reign'd ;
Nor trader villains foul'd the Savage mind ;
Nor Avarice pin'd for boundlefs breadth of land ;
Nor, with flow death, the wretches been confign'd.   310
To India's curfe, that poifons half mankind !
Then, O divine Religion ! torture's blaze
Lefs frequent round thy tender heart had twin'd ;
On the wild wigwam peace had caft it's rays,
And the tremendous whoop had chang'd to hymns of praife. 315

Fierce, dark, and jealous, is the exotic foul,
That, cell'd in fecret, rules the favage breaft.
There treacherous thoughts of gloomy vengeance roll,
And deadly deeds of malice unconfefs'd ;
The viper's poifon rankling in it's neft.   320
Behind his tree, each Indian aims unfeen :
No fweet oblivion foothes the hate imprefs'd :

Years fleet in vain: in vain realms intervene :
The victim's blood alone can quench the flames within.

Their knives the tawny tribes in flaughter fteep,   325
When men, miftruftlefs, think them diftant far ;
And, when blank midnight fhrouds the world in fleep,
The murderous yell announces firft the war.
In vain fweet fmiles compel the fiends to fpare ;
Th' unpitied victim fcreams, in tortures dire ;   330
The life-blood ftains the virgin's bofom bare ;
Cherubic infants, limb by limb expire ;
And filver'd Age finks down in flowly-curling fire.

Yet favages are men.   With glowing heat,
Fix'd as their hatred, friendfhip fills their mind ;   335
By acts with juftice, and with truth, replete,
Their iron breafts to foftnefs are inclin'd.
But when could War of converts boaft refin'd ?
Or when Revenge to peace and fweetnefs move ?
His heart, man yields alone to actions kind ;   340
His faith, to creeds, whofe foundnefs virtues prove,
Thawn in the April fun, and opening ftill to love.

Senate auguft ! that fway'ft Columbian climes,
Form'd of the wife, the noble, and humane,
Caft back the glance through long-afcending times,   245
And think what nations fill'd the weftern plain.
Where are they now ? What thoughts the bofom pain,
From mild Religion's eye how ftreams the tear,
To fee fo far outfpread the wafte of man,
And afk " How fell the myriads, HEAVEN plac'd here !"   350.
Reflect, be juft, and feel for Indian woes fevere.

But ceafe, foul Calumny ! with footy tongue,
No more the glory of our fires belie.
They felt, and they redrefs'd, each nation's wrong ;
Even Pequod foes they view'd with generous eye ;   355
And, pierc'd with injuries keen, that Virtue try,

The favage faith, and friendfhip, ftrove to gain :
And, had no bafe Canadian fiends been nigh,
Even now foft Peace had fmil'd on every plain,
And tawny nations liv'd, and own'd MESSIAH's reign.) 360

" Amid a circling marfh, expanded wide,
To a lone hill the Pequods wound their way;
And none, but Heaven, the manfion had defcried,
Clofe-tangled, wild, impervious to the day ;
But one poor wanderer, loitering long aftray,   365
Wilder'd in labyrinths of pathlefs wood,
In a tall tree embower'd, obfcurely lay :
Strait fummon'd down, the trembling fuppliant fhow'd
Where lurk'd his vanifh'd friends, within their drear abode."

" To death, the murderers were anew requir'd,   370
A pardon proffer'd, and a peace affur'd ;
And, though with vengeful heat their foes were fir'd,
Their lives, their freedom, and their lands, fecur'd.
Some yielding heard. In faftnefs ftrong immur'd,
The reft the terms refus'd, with brave difdain,   375
Near, and more near, the peaceful Herald lur'd ;
Then bade a fhower of arrows round him rain,
And wing'd him fwift, from danger, to the diftant plain."

" Through the fole, narrow way, to vengeance led,
To final fight our generous heroes drew ;   380
And Stoughton now had pafs'd the moor's black fhade,
When hell's terrific region fcream'd anew.
Undaunted, on their foes they fiercely flew ;
As fierce, the dufky warriors crowd the fight ;
Defpair infpires ; to combat's face they glue ;   185
With groans, and fhouts, they rage, unknowing flight,
And clofe their fullen eyes, in fhades of endlefs night."

Indulge, my native land ! indulge the tear,
That fteals, impaffion'd, o'er a nation's doom :

To me each twig, from Adam's stock, is near,   390
And sorrows fall upon an Indian's tomb.
And, O ye Chiefs! in yonder starry home,
Accept the humble tribute of this rhyme.
Your gallant deeds, in Greece, or haughty Rome,
By Maro sung, or Homer's harp sublime,   395
Had charm'd the world's wide round, and triumph'd over time.

END OF THE FOURTH PART.

N

GREENFIELD HILL:

A

POEM.

THE ARGUMENT.

SUBJECT introduced. *Description of a happy village in New England. Character of the Clergyman. He gives his last advice, and blessing, to his Parishioners—recites his past, affectionate and faithful labours for their salvation, and proposes to close them with his last exhortation—estimates the pleasures of sin, and the value of the present life, and urges them to seek eternal life—informs them, that two endless journeys lie before them—of virtue, which guides to happiness; and of sin, which terminates in misery—and describes the nature of both. As means of salvation, he exhorts them to read the Bible, with diligence and care; to frequent public worship; to establish family religion, in their houses; religiously to educate their children; and to abound in all the duties of charity. He further informs them, that all things are labouring to promote this great purpose; recites to them the affectionate invitations of the Redeemer; and represents his own future happiness, as increased by their salvation. Conclusion.*

GREENFIELD HILL.

PART V.

THE CLERGYMAN's ADVICE TO THE VILLAGERS.

WHILE thus, from winter's tranfient death,
The world revives to life, and breath;
While round me all your bleffings rife,
And peace, and plenty, greet my eyes;
Ah fay! ye children of my care,   5
Of every wifh, of every prayer,
Ordain'd my facred charge below,
The fource of joy, the fource of woe,
Say, fhall my heart on landfchapes mufe,
And fcenes of nobler kind refufe;   10
Alone for haplefs Indians feel;
Forget, in others woes, your weal,
Unmov'd, behold your footfteps roam,
Nor guide the wayward pilgrim home?
No, let the moral fong prevail;   15
Lift, lift, to truth's perfuafive tale.
While Heaven, by hoary Wifdom fung,
Infpires my heart, and tunes my tongue,

'Oh hear, and from perdition rife,
And point your pathway to the fkies !　　　　　20

Where weftern Albion's happy clime
Still brightens to the eye of time,
A village lies. In all his round,
The fun a fairer never found.
The woods were tall, the hillocks green,　　25
The vallies laugh'd the hills between,
Thro' fairy meads the rivers roll'd,
The meadows flower'd in vernal gold,
The days were bright, the mornings fair,
And evening lov'd to linger there.　　　　30
·There, twinn'd in brilliant fields above,
Sweet fifters ! fported Peace and Love ;
While Virtue, like a blufhing bride,
Seren'd, and brighten'd, at their fide.

At diftance from that happy way,　　　　35
The path of fenfual Pleafure lay,
Afar Ambition's fummit rofe,
And Avarice dug his mine of woes.

The place, with eaft and weftern fides,
A wide and verdant ftreet divides :　　　　40
And here the houfes fac'd the day,
And there the lawns in beauty lay.
There, turret-crown'd, and central, ftood
A neat, and folemn houfe of God.
Acrofs the way, beneath the fhade,　　　　45
Two elms with fober filence fpread,
The Preacher liv'd. O'er all the place
His manfion caft a Sunday grace ;
Dumb ftillnefs fate the fields around ;
His garden feem'd a hallow'd ground ;　　50
Swains ceas'd to laugh aloud, when near,
And fchool-boys never fported there.

In the fame mild, and temperate zone,
Twice twenty years, his courfe had run,
His locks of flowing filver fpread,   55
A crown of glory o'er his head.
His face, the image of his mind,
With grave, and furrow'd wifdom fhin'd;
Not cold; but glowing ftill, and bright;
Yet glowing with October light: 60
As evening blends, with beauteous ray,
Approaching night with fhining day.

His Cure his thoughts engrofs'd alone:
For them his painful courfe was run:
To blefs, to fave, his only care;   65
To chill the guilty foul with fear;
To point the pathway to the fkies,
And teach, and urge, and aid, to rife;
Where ftrait, and difficult to keep,
It climbs, and climbs, o'er Virtue's fteep.   70

As now the evening of his day,
Retiring, fmil'd it's warning ray;
He heard, in angel-whifpers, come,
The welcome voice, that call'd him home.
The little flock he nurs'd fo long,   75
And charm'd with mercy's fweeteft fong,
His heart with ftrong affections warm'd,
His love provok'd, his fears alarm'd—
Like him, who freed the chofen band,
Like him, who op'd the promis'd land,   80
His footfteps verging on the grave,
His blefling thus the Prophet gave.

" O priz'd beyond expreffion here,
As fons belov'd, as daughters dear,
Your Father's dying voice receive,   85
My counfels hear, obey, and live!"

" For you my ceaselefs toils ye know,
My care, my faithfulnefs, and woe.
For you I breath'd unnumber'd prayers ;
For you I fhed unnumber'd tears ;   90
To living fprings the thirfty led,
The hungry cheer'd with living bread ;
Of grief allay'd the piercing fmart,
And footh'd with balm the doubting heart ;
The wayward flock forbade to roam,   95
And brought the wandering lambkin home."

" And now, my toils, my duties done,
My crown of endlefs glory won,
Ev'n while, invited to the fkies,
My wing begins through heaven to rife,   100
One folemn labour ftill is due,
To clofe a life, confum'd for you."

" Say, what the gain ? Oh fearch, and fay!—
To tread the fatal, fenfual way ?
To briftle down in pleafure's ftye ?   105
To heap up filver, mountains high ?
With guilt to climb, with anguifh keep,
Ambition's proud, and painful fteep ?
Should earth for your enjoyment roll,
Can earth redeem the deathlefs foul ?"   110

" This little life, my children! fay,
What is it ? A departing day ;
An April morn, with froft behind ;
A bubble, burfting on the wind ;
A dew, exhal'd beneath the fun ;   115
A tale rehears'd ; a vifion gone."

" How oft too, in the bright career,
Which Pride, and Pleafure wanton here,
While Hope expands her painted wing,
And all around is health, and fpring ;   120

How oft refounds the awful knell,
That feals to life a long farewell,
" " Thou fool! diffolv'd in guilt and fenfe,
This night, thy foul is fummon'd hence." "

" Yet on this little life depend   125
Bleffings, and woes, which cannot end.
For Faith and Penitence below,
Immortal life and rapture glow;
For harden'd guilt, eternal ire,
And waves, that furge unfathom'd fire."   130

" Then rife from death's benumbing fleep!
See, fpread beneath, the yawning deep!
Oh rife! and let falvation call
Your time, your thoughts, and talents all."

" Two only paths betore you fpread;   135
And long the way, your feet muft tread.
This ftrait, and rough, and narrow, lies
The courfe direct to yonder fkies.
And now o'er hills, on hills, you climb,
Deferted paths, and cliffs fublime;   140
And now thro' folitudes you go,
Thro' vales of care, and ftreams of woe.
Tho' oft you wander fad, forlorn,
The mark of fpite, the butt of fcorn;
Yet your's the fweets, that cannot cloy,   145
The Saviour's peace, the Seraph's joy;
While nurture Heaven itfelf fupplies,
And fruits depend, and fprings arife;
And Health and Temperance, fifters gay,
Defpife the leffening length of way;   150
And fweet, tho' rare, companions fmile,
Deceive the road, and lofe the toil;
And Hope ftill points th' approaching goal,
As magnets tremble to the pole."

O

" As now at hand the realm appears,   155
Where pains retire, and cares, and tears,
Then fmooths the rough, the rude refines,
The defert blooms, the fteep declines;
Then bright, and brighter, fpreads the plain,
Where Love begins her vernal reign.   160
And fweet as mufic of the fkies,
When hymns of blefs'd Redemption rife,
Your FATHER's welcome hails you home;
The LAMB, the SPIRIT bid you come;
And all the Family around   165
Salute you to the blifsful ground,
The heirs of life, the fons of God,
And trophies of their SAVIOUR's blood."

" Full wide the other path extends,
And round, and round, ferpentine bends.   170
To fenfe, bewitching flow'rets bloom,
And charm, and cheat, with ftrange perfume;
Fruits hang diffolving poifon nigh,
And purpling death inchants the eye.
Companions, frolickfome and gay,   175
Laugh jocund on the downward way,
With wiles entice a thoughtlefs throng,
And, blinded, lead the blind along,
Where fmooth, and treacherous, and fteep,
It flides, impending, to the deep."   180

" At length, where Death dominion holds,
A wide and gloomy gate unfolds—
Thro' folitudes immenfely fpread,
The mourning manfions of the dead,
A dreary tomb, that knows no bound,   185
A midnight hung eternal round,
Their journey winds—No friend appears
To dry the ftream of endlefs tears.

Sweet Hope, that footh'd their pains before,
Returns to foothe their pains no more.   190
Thro' the long night, the eye looks on,
But meets with no returning fun ;
While Peace refigns to blank Defpair,
And light is chang'd to darknefs there."

 " Then rife, and let falvation call   195
Your time, your thoughts, your talents all !"

 " For this, the facred page explore,
Confult, and ponder, o'er and o'er ;
The words of endlefs life difcern ;
The way, the means, the motives, learn ;   200
The hopes, the promifes, enjoy,
That ne'er deceive, that cannot cloy ;
Alarms to Guilt's obdurate mind ;
Perennial blifs to Faith affign'd ;
The precepts, by MESSIAH given ;   205
His life, the image bright of Heaven ;
His death, felf-ruin'd man to fave ;
His rife, primitial, from the grave ;
Beyond all other love, his love ;
His name, all other names above.   210
All duties to be learn'd, or done,
All comforts to be gain'd, or known,
To do, to gain, unceafing ftrive,
The book of books explore, and live,"

 " When fmiles the Sabbath's genial morn,   215
Inftinctive to the Temple turn ;
Your houfholds round you thither bring,
Sweet off'ring to the SAVIOUR KING.
There, on the mercy-feat, he fhines,
Receives our fouls, forgets our fins,   220
And welcomes, with refiftlefs charms,
Submitting rebels to his arms.

That chofen, blefs'd, accepted day
Oh never never caft away !"

" Let order round your houfes reign,   225
Religion rule, and peace fuftain ;
Each morn, each eve, your prayers arife,
As incenfe fragrant, to the fkies ;
In beauteous groupe, your children join,
And fervants fhare the work divine :   230
The voice, as is the intereft, one,
And one the blefling wreftled down."

" Each toil devote, each care, and pain,
Your children for the fkies to. train.
Allure, reprove, inftruct, reclaim,   235
Alarm, and warn, commend, and blame;
To virtue force with gentle fway,
And guide, and lead, yourfelves, the way.
Teach them, profanenefs, falfhood, fraud,
Abufe to man, affronts to GOD,   240
All things impure, obfcene, debas'd,
Tho' oft with high examples grac'd,
To fhun beyond the adder's breath,
When hifling inftantaneous death ;
But juftice, truth, and love, to prize,   245
Beyond the tranfports of the fkies."

" Teach them, that, brighter than the fun,
Th' All-fearching Eye looks flaming on,
Each thought, each word, each act, defcries,
And fees the guilty motives rife ;   250
A Witnefs, and a Judge, that day,
Whofe light fhall every heart difplay.
Live what you teach—the heavenly SEER,
Who fpake, as man ne'er fpake, when here,
Taught all things juft, and wife, and true,   255
Shone, a divine example too."

" To all, around, your bleſſings lend,
The ſick relieve, the poor befriend,
The ſad conſole, the weak ſuſtain,
And ſoothe the wounded ſpirit's pain   260
To you, think every bleſſing given,
To ſhed abroad the alms of HEAVEN,
To blunt the ſtings of human woe,
And build his kingdom, here below.
Let gentle Peace around you reign,   265
Her influence ſpread, her cauſe ſuſtain :
To railing, anſwers mild return ;
Let love, oppos'd to anger, burn :
Contention, ere begun, ſuppreſs,
And bid the voice of party ceaſe.   270
The taleful tongue, the meddling mind,
The jealous eye, the heart unkind,
Far diſtant, far, from you remove ;
But ope your doors to Truth, and Love :
The meek eſteem, the humble praiſe,   275
And Merit from her footſtool raiſe."

" By every act of peace, and love,
Thus win your way to climes above.
In this great work, ſee all things ſtrive !
Nature toils that you may live :   280

" Lo, to aid you to the ſkies,
Seaſons roll, and ſuns ariſe ;
Promis'd, ſee the ſeed-time come,
And the harveſt ſhouted home !"

" All things, in their ſolemn round,   285
Morn, with peace and beauty crown'd,
Eve, with ſweet, returning reſt,
Toil, with health and plenty bleſs'd,
Help you on the aſcending road,
Pointing, leading, ſtill to God :   290

Joys to endlefs rapture charm;
Woes, of endlefs woe, alarm."

" All things toil, that you may live——
Rulers peace and freedom give:
Seers diviner peace proclaim,   295
Glorious to th' Unutter'd NAME,
Good, to guilty mortals given,
Source of endlefs joy to heaven."

" See the Sabbath's peaceful morn,
(Sabbaths ftill for you return),   300
Opes the Temple to your feet,
Chaunting founds of Seraphs fweet——
" Heaven unfolds, and GOD is near,
Sinners hafte, and enter here"——
Grace and truth, from worlds above,   305
Fruits of fuffering, dying love,
From the SACRED SPIRIT come,
Wilder'd flocks inviting home."

" Hark, what living mufic plays!
Catch the themes of heavenly praife;   310
Themes, that tune feraphic ftrings,
Notes, the blefs'd REDEEMER fings."

" " Rife, my fons, and hither hafte!
Wintry time is overpafs'd.
See afar the rains have flown!   315
See immortal fpring begun!
Streams with life and rapture flow;
Fruits with life and rapture glow;
Love the door of life unbars;
Triumphs crown your finifh'd wars: 320
Fondly wait impatient fkies,
O'er you to renew their joys." "

" " Are you naked? here behold
Robes of light, and crowns of gold!

Famiſh'd ? an eternal feaſt !　　　　　325
Weary ? everliving reſt !
Friendleſs ? an ALMIGHTY FRIEND !
Hopeleſs ? tranſports ne'er to end !" "

" " Children, penitents, ariſe ;
Haſten to your native ſkies :　　　　330
Your arrival all things ſing ;
Angels meet you on the wing ;
Saints with fairer beauty ſhine ;
Brighter years in heaven begin ;
Round the SUN, that lights the ſkies,　335
More refulgent glories riſe." "

" Thus, O my ſons ! MESSIAH's voice
Allures to never dying joys.
That voice of endleſs love receive ;
Thoſe counſels hear, obey, and live."　340

" Thus, from the climes beyond the tomb
If GOD permit my ſoul to come,
Again my little flock to view,
To watch, and warn, and quicken you,
With tranſport ſhall my boſom glow,　345
To ſee each houſe an heaven below,
My ſons ambitious of the ſkies,
And future ſaints, and angels riſe.
And O, what brighter bliſs ſhall bloom,
To hail you victors o'er the tomb ;　350
To guide you, all th' unmeaſur'd way,
And welcome to the gates of day ;
To hear your bleſſed Euge ſound,
And ſee th' immortals ſmile around ;
To ſtand, to ſhine, by you confeſs'd　355
Your friend your earthly ſaviour bleſs'd ;
To mingle joys, all joys above,
And warm with ever-bright'ning love !"

He fpoke. The filial tear around,
Refponfive, trickled to the found ;
He faw their hearts to wifdom won,
And felt his final duty done—
" Jesus ! my foul receive"—he cried,
And fmil'd, and bow'd his head, and died.

360

END OF THE FIFTH PART.

GREENFIELD HILL:

A

POEM.

THE ARGUMENT.

*INTRODUCTION. Farmer introduced. Villagers aſ-
ſembled. He recommends to them an induſtrious and œconomical
life, the careful education and government of their children,
and particularly the eſtabliſhment of good habits in early life;
enjoins upon them the offices of good neighbourhood, the avoidance
of litigation, and the careful cultivation of parochial harmony.
Concluſion.*

GREENFIELD HILL.

PART VI.

THE FARMER's ADVICE TO THE VILLAGERS.

———

YE children of my fondeſt care,
With tendereſt love, and frequent prayer,
This ſolemn charge, my voice has given,
To prompt, and guide, your ſteps to heaven.
Your preſent welfare now demands   5
A different tribute, from my hands.

Not long ſince liv'd a Farmer plain,
Intent to gather honeſt gain,
Laborious, prudent, thrifty, neat,
Of judgment ſtrong, experience great,   10
In ſolid homeſpun clad, and tidy,
And with no coxcomb learning giddy.
Daily, to hear his maxims found,
Th' approaching neighbours flock'd around ;
Daily they ſaw his counſels prove   15
The ſource of union, peace, and love,
The means of prudence, and of wealth,
Of comfort, cheerfulneſs, and health :

And all, who follow'd his advice,
Appear'd more profperous, as more wife,　　　　20

 Wearied, at length, with many a call,
The fage refolv'd to fummon all :
And gathering, on a pleafant monday,
A crowd, not always feen on funday,
Curious to hear, while hard they prefs'd him,　　25
In friendly terms, he thus addrefs'd 'em.

 " My friends, you have my kindeft wifhes ;
Pray think a neighbour not officious,
While thus, to teach you how to live,
My very beft advice I give."　　　　30

 " And firft, *induftrious* be your lives ;
Alike employ'd yourfelves, and wives :
Your children, join'd in labour gay,
With fomething ufeful fill each day.
Thofe little times of leifure fave,　　　　35
Which moft men lofe, and all men have ;
The half days, when a job is done ;
The whole days, when a ftorm is on.
Few know, without a ftrict account,
To what thefe little times amount :　　　　40
If wafted, while the fame your coft,
The fums, you might have earn'd, are loft."

 " Learn *fmall things never to defpife :*
You little think how faft they rife.
A rich reward the mill obtains,　　　　45
'Tho' but two quarts a bufhel gains :
Still rolling on it's fteady rounds,
The farthings foon are turn'd to pounds."

 " Nor *think a life of toil fevere :*
No life has bleflings fo fincere.　　　　50
It's meals fo lufcious, fleep fo fweet,
Such vigorous limbs, fuch health complete,

A mind fo active, brifk, and gay,
As his, who toils the livelong day.
A life of floth drags hardly on;   55
Suns fet too late, and rife too foon;
Youth, manhood, age, all linger flow,
To him, who nothing has to do.
The drone, a nuifance to the hive,
Stays, but can fcarce be faid to live;   60
And well the bees, thofe judges wife,
Plague, chafe, and fting him, 'till he dies.
Lawrence, like him, tho' fav'd from hanging,
Yet every day deferves a banging."

" Let *order* o'er your time prefide,   65
And *method* all your bufinefs guide.
Early begin, and end, your toil;
Nor let great tafks your hands embroil.
One thing at once, be ftill begun,
Contriv'd, refolv'd, purfued, and done.   70
Hire not, for what yourfelves can do;
And fend not, when yourfelves can go;
Nor, 'till to-morrow's light, delay
What might as well be done to-day.
By fteady efforts all men thrive,   75
And long by moderate labour live;
While eager toil, and anxious care,
Health, ftrength, and peace, and life, impair."

" What thus your hands with labour earn,
To fave, be now your next concern.   80
Whate'er to health, or real ufe,
Or true enjoyment, will conduce,
Ufe freely, and *with pleafure* ufe;
But ne'er the gifts of HEAVEN abufe:
I joy to fee your treafur'd ftores,   85
Which fmiling Plenty copious pours;

Your cattle fleek, your poultry fine,
Your cider in the tumbler fhine,
Your tables, fmoking from the hoard,
And children fmiling round the board.　　　90
All rights to ufe in you confpire;
The labourer's worthy of his hire.
Ne'er may that hated day arrive,
When worfe yourfelves, or your's, fhall live;
Your drefs, your lodging, or your food,　　　95
Be lefs abundant, neat, or good;
Your dainties all to market go,
To feaft the epicure, and beau;
But ever on your tables ftand,
Proofs of a free and happy land."　　　100

　"Yet ftill, with prudence, wear, and tafte;
Ufe what you pleafe, but nothing wafte:
On little, better far to live,
Than, poor and pitied, much furvive.
Like ants, lay fomething up in ftore,　　　105
Againft the winter of threefcore.
Difeafe may long your ftrength annoy;
Weaknefs and pain your limbs deftroy;
On forrow's bed your houfholds lie;
Your debtors fail, your cattle die;　　　110
Your crops untimely feafons kill,
And life be worn with many an ill."

　"Lo too, your little flocks demand
Much from the kind parental hand;
Your fons or learning, trades, or farms;　　　115
Your daughter's portions, with their charms:
From prudence, this provifion flows,
And all, from little favings, grows."

　"And, O ye fair! this toil demands
The efforts of your faithful hands.　　　120

If wealth, your hufband's hearts are wifhing,
Of you, they firft muft afk permiffion.
By HEAVEN conjoin'd, to gain, and have,
'Tis their's to earn; 'tis yours to fave :
Whatever from their labour grows,   125
Careful, you keep, but, heedlefs, lofe."

" 'Tis folly in th' extreme, *to till*
Extenfive fields, and till them ill.
The farmer, pleas'd, may boaft aloud
His bufhels fown, his acres plough'd;   130
And, pleas'd, indulge the cheering hope,
That time will bring a plenteous crop.
Shrewd Common-fenfe fits laughing by,
And fees his hopes abortive die :
For, when maturing feafons fmile,   135
Thin fheaves fhall difappoint his toil.
Advis'd, this empty pride expel;
Till little, and that little well.
Of taxes, fencing, toil, no more,
Your ground requires, when rich, than poor;   140
And more one fertile acre yields,
Than the huge breadth of barren fields.
That mould, the leaves, for ages, fpread,
Is, long fince, with the forefts, fled;
That flender ploughing, trifling care,   145
No longer will your fields prepare.
Some new manure muft now be found;
Some better culture fit the ground.
Oft turn the foil to feel the weather;
Manure from every quarter gather,   150
Weeds, afhes, Paris-plaifter, lime,
Marle, fea-weed, and the harbour flime.
Like Germans bid your acres thrive;
But not like ftinting Germans live.

" Let *every grafs of kindly feed*
Exterminate the noifome weed;

The clover round your paftures blow ;
The rye-grafs o'er your meadows bow :
Hence the rich mow your barns fhall fill ;
Hence with rich green your paftures fmile ;   160
The ox, untir'd, his toil fuftain,
And fat fteers frifk it, o'er the plain."

  " *Your herds feed well, increafe, amend,*
And from the wintery ftorm defend.
No fource will furer profit give,   165
Or furnifh eafier means to live.
The grazier hugs his cool retreat,
And fmiles, to fee the farmer fweat ;
To fee much labour little yield,
The gleanings of a worne-out field ;   170
While gliftening beeves around him fport,
And drovers to his houfe refort ;
Manur'd, huge fwarths his meadows load,
And heavy harvefts proudly nod."

  " Let *ufeful flocks* your care demand,   175
Beft riches of the happy land.
From them, fhall fwell the fleecy ftore,
And want, and rags, depart your door ;
Your daughters find a fweet employ,
And, finging, turn the wheel with joy :   180
With homefpun rich the loom be gay ;
Your houfholds clad in bright array ;
And female toil more profit yield,
Than half the labours of the field."

  " When firft the market offers well,   185
At once your yearly produce fell.
A higher price you wait in vain,
And ten times lofe, where once you gain.
The dog, that at the fhadow caught,
Mifs'd all he had, and all he fought.   190

Lefs, day by day, your ftore will grow,
Gone, you fcarce know or when, or how;
Intereft will eat, while you delay,
And vermin fteal your hopes away.
In parcels fold, in ways unknown,   195
It melts, and, unobferv'd, is gone.
No folid purpofe driblets aid,
Spent, and forgot, as foon as paid :
The fum, a year's whole earnings yield,
Will pay a debt, or buy a field."   200

" *In time,* whate'er your needs require,
Lay in, of clothing, food, or fire.
Your cellars, barns, and granaries fill;
Your wood, in winter, round you pile :
Let fpring ne'er fee th' exhaufted mow,   205
Or oxen faint, before the plough ;
Nor fummer, when it's hurries come,
Your wood, in harveft, carted home."

" Along the fide of floping hills,
Conduct your numerous living rills.   210
Thence bid them, fweetly-wandering, flow,
To wake the grafs, in fields below.
Rich meadows in their courfe fhall fpring,
And mowers whet the fcythe, and fing."

" Look round, and fee *your wood's decay'd,*   215
Your fuel fcarce, your timber fled.
What groves remain with care enclofe,
Nor e'er to biting herds expofe.
Your ftore with planted nuts renew,
And acorns o'er each barren ftrew.   220
Tho' fpring now fmiles, yet winter's blaft
Will foon the frozen fkies o'ercaft ;
And, pinch'd, your children crowding nigher,
Hang fhivering o'er the fcanty fire :

Q

Roufe ! your reluctant floth o'ercome,   225
And bid reviving forefts bloom."

" Yearly the houfe, the barn, the fence,
Demand *much care,* and *fome expence.*
Small fums, in time, with prudence paid,
Will profit more than great, delay'd :   230
Each year's decays in time repair,
Nor foolifh wafte, thro' want of care."

" *Neat be your farms :* 'tis long confefs'd,
The neateft farmers are the beft.
Each bog, and marfh, induftrious drain,   235
Nor let vile balks deform the plain ;
No bufhes on your headlands grow,
Nor briars a floven's culture fhow.
Neat be your barns ; your houfes neat ;
Your doors be clean ; your court-yards fweet ; 240
No mofs the fheltering roof infhroud ;
No wooden panes the window cloud ;
No filthy kennel foully flow ;
Nor weeds with rankling poifon grow :
But fhades expand, and fruit-trees bloom,   245
And flowering fhrubs exhale perfume.
With pales, your garden circle round ;
Defend, enrich, and clean, the ground :
Prize high this pleafing, ufeful rood,
And fill with vegetable good."   250

" *With punctual hand your taxes pay,*
Nor put far off the evil day.
How foon to an enormous fize,
Taxes, fucceeding taxes, rife !
How eafy, one by one, difcharg'd !   255
How hardly, in the mafs enlarg'd !
How humbling the intrufive dun !
How faft, how far, th' expences run !

Fees, advertifements, travel, coft,
And that fad end of all, the poft !　　　　　260
This gulph of quick perdition flee,
And live, from duns and bailiffs free."

" In *merchants' books, from year to year,*
Be cautious how your names appear.
How faft their little items count !　　　　　265
How great, beyond your hopes, th' amount !
When fhelves, o'er fhelves, inviting ftand,
And wares allure, on either hand ;
While round, you turn enchanted eyes,
And feel a thoufand wants arife,　　　　　270
(Ye young, ye fair, thefe counfels true
Are penn'd for all, but moft for you),
Ere Fancy lead your hearts aftray,
Think of the means you have, to pay ;
What wants are nature's ; fancy's what ;　　　275
What will yield real good, when bought ;
What certain, future means you find,
To cancel contracts, left behind ;
What means to make the firft of May
To you, and your's, a welcome day."　　　　280

" To you, let *each returning fpring*
That day of certain reckoning bring :
All debts to cancel, books t' adjuft,
And check the wild career of truft.
From frequent reckonings friendfhip grows,　　285
And peace, and fweet communion, flows."

" Meanwhile, of all your toil, and care,
Your children claim the largeft fhare.
In health, and ficknefs, much they need,
To nurfe, to watch, to clothe, and feed ;　　290
Their education much demands
From faithful hearts, and active hands."

" Firſt be *their health* your conſtant care ;
Give them to breathe the freeſt air :
Their food be neither rich, nor dainty,   295
But plain, and clean, and good, and plenty :
Their clothes, let changing feafons rule,
In winter warm, in fummer cool,
In your own houfes fpun, and dy'd,
For comfort made, and not for pride.   300
Hardy, not fuffering, be their life,
With heat, and cold, and ſtorm, at ſtrife ;
Accuſtom'd common ills to bear,
To fmile at danger, laugh at fear,
Troubles to brave, with hardy breaſt,   305
And feek, thro' toilfome action, reſt.
Teach them each *manly art to prize,*
And bafe effem'nacy defpife,
Teach them to wreſtle, leap, and run,
To win the palm, and prize it, won ;   310
To feek, in acts like thefe, and find
A nervous frame, and vigorous mind."

" *My country's youth, I fee with pain,*
The cuſtoms of their fires difdain,
Quit the bold paſtimes of the green,   315
That ſtrengthen ſtriplings into men,
Grovel in inns, at cards, and dice,
The means of foul difeafe, and vice,
And waſte, in gaming, drink, and ſtrife,
Health, honour, fame, and peace, and life."   320

" *With gentler hand, your daughters train,*
The houfewife's various arts to gain ;
O'er fcenes domeſtic to prefide ;
The needle, wheel, and ſhuttle, guide ;
The peacock's gaudry to defpife,   325
And view vain fports with parents' eyes ;

On things of ufe to fix the heart,
And gild, with every graceful art.
Teach them, with neateft, fimpleft drefs,
A neat, and lovely mind t' exprefs;   330
Th' alluring female mien to wear;
Gently to foothe corroding care;
Bid life with added pleafure glow,
And fweetly charm the bed of woe.
To fhow, the giddy fair-one train'd,   335
With every ugly fpot is ftain'd;
While fhe, who lives to worth, and duty,
Shines forth, in Wifdom's eye, a beauty."

   " *With fteady hand yonr houfhold fway,*
And ufe them always to obey.   340
Always their worthy acts commend;
Always againft their faults contend;
The mind inform; the confcience move;
And blame, with tendernefs, and love.
When round they flock, and fmile, and tell   345
Their lambkin fports, and infant weal,
Nor foolifh laugh, nor fret, nor frown;
But all their little interefts own;
Like them, thofe trifles ferious deem,
And daily witnefs your efteem: 350
Yourfelves their beft friends always prove,
For filial duty fprings from love.
Teach them, *with confidence t' impart,*
Each fecret purpofe of the heart: 355
Thrice happy parents, children blefs'd,
Of mutual confidence poffefs'd!
Such parents fhall their children fee
From vice, and fhame, and anguifh, free."

   " *Correct not, 'til the coming day*
Has fann'd refentment's heat away.   360

When paffion rules, 'tis fear obeys ;
But duty ferves, when reafon fways.
In earlieft years, the rod will mend ;
In later, fails to reach the end.
Still vary : let neglect, difgrace,   365
Confinement, cenfure, find their place.
Convince, ere you correct, and prove
You punifh, not from rage, but love ;
And teach them, with perfuafion mild,
You hate the fault, but love the child."   370

" *All difcipline*, as facts atteft,
In private minifter'd is beft.
Vex'd to be feen difgrac'd, and fham'd,
His paffion rous'd, his pride inflam'd,
Your child his guilt with care conceals,   375
And pertly talks, and ftoutly feels ;
From truth, with fwift declenfion flies,
To arts, equivocations, lies ;
And fullen broods, with fad defign,
O'er fweet revenge of future fin.   380
Alone, before the parents bar,
His confcience with himfelf at war,
Of pride, and petulance, bereft,
Without a hope, or refuge, left,
He fhrinks, beneath a father's eye,   385
And feels his firm perverfenefs die ;
Reveres the love, his fighs implore,
And grateful turns, to fin no more."

" *On uniformity depends*
All government, that gains its ends.   390
The fame things always praife, and blame,
Your laws, and conduct, be the fame."

" Let no *difcouragement* deter,
Nor *floth* this daily tafk defer.

Sloth and difcouragement deftroy   395
The children's weal, the parents' joy.
For one, who labor lothes, we find
Ten thoufand lothing toil of mind,
That clofe attention, careful tho't,
With every real blefling fraught.   400
Early the ftubborn child transgreffes;
Denies it; nor, 'till forc'd, confeffes:
The fault, tho' punifh'd, he renews;
New punifhment the fault purfues:
His heart by nature prone to fin,   405
Agen he wounds you, and agen;
Amaz'd, difhearten'd, in defpair,
To fee fo fruitlefs all your care,
And wearied, by fuch fix'd attention
To crimes, that fuffer no prevention,   410
Reluctant, by degrees, you yield,
And leave him mafter of the field."

" Then with fond hope, that reafon's fway
Will win him from his faults away,
For decent power, alone you ftrive,   415
Refign'd, if decently he'll live."

" Vain hope! by reafon's power alone,
From guilt, no heart was ever won.
Decent, not good, may reafon make him;
By reafon, crimes will ne'er forfake him.   420
As weeds, felf-fown, demand no toil,
But flourifh in their native foil,
Root deep, grow high, with vigour bloom,
And fend forth poifon, for perfume;
So faults, inborn, fpontaneous rife,   425
And daily wax in ftrength, and fize,
Ripen, with neither toil, nor care,
And choke each germ of virtue there.

Virtues, like plants of nobler kind,
Transferred from regions more refin'd,   430
The gardener's careful hand muft fow;
His culturing hand muft bid them grow;
Rains gently fhower; fkies foftly fhine,
And bleffings fall, from realms divine."

"Much time, and pain, and toil, and care,
Muft virtue's habits plant, and rear:
Habits alone thro' life endure,
Habits alone your child fecure :
To thefe be all your labours given;
To thefe, your fervent prayers to HEAVEN.   440
Nor faint, a thoufand trials o'er,
To fee your pains effect no more;
Love, duty, intereft, bid you ftrive;
Contend, and yield not, while you live;
And know, for all your labours pafs'd,   445
Your eyes fhall fee a crop, at laft.
The fmith befide his anvil ftands,
The lump of filver in his hands,
A thoufand ftrokes with patience gives,
And ftill unform'd the work perceives;   450
A thoufand, and a thoufand more,
Unfinifh'd leaves it as before;
Yet, though, from each, no print is found,
Still toiling on his fteady round,
He fees the ductile mafs refine,
And in a beauteous veffel fhine."

"*Taverns, and fhops, and lounging places,*
Vile comrades, gaming tables, races,
Where youth to vice, and ruin, run,
Teach them, as pits of death, to fhun.   460
At nine, when founds the warning bell,
Ufe them to bid their fports farewell;

Health, order, temperance, every joy;
As blafts, untimely hours deftroy;
At thefe dread hours, in places vile,   465
Where all things tempt, betray, defile,
Abroad, to every ill they roam,
But peace, and fafety, find at home."

" *From licens'd talk their tongues reftrain*,
And bridle, with difcretion's rein ;   470
Safety, and peace, referve affords ;
But evil hides in many words.
All wond'rous ftories bid them fhun,
And the *pernicious love of fun* ;
In lies, great ftories ever end,   475
And fun will every vice befriend.
What fports of real ufe you find,
To brace the form, or nerve the mind,
Freely indulge ; fuch fports, as thefe,
Will profit youth, as well as pleafe.   480
But from all arts and tricks dehort,
And check th' exceffive love of fport.
All buzzing tales, of private life,
All fcandals, form'd on houfhold ftrife,
The idle chatterings of the ftreet,   485
Early forbid them to repeat ;
But teach them, kindnefs, praife, and truth,
Alone become the voice of youth."

" *Their hearts with foft affections warm ;*
Their tafte, to gentle manners form :   490
Let manly aims their bofoms fire,
And fweet civility infpire.
Bid them the ftranger kindly greet,
The friend with faithful friendfhip meet,
And charm of life the little fpan,   495
By general courtefy to man."

R

" *Teach them to reverence righteous fway*,
With life defend, with love obey;
Nor join that wretched band of fcoffers,
Who rail at every man in office.   500
With freedom's warmth their fouls infpire,
And light their brave forefathers' fire.
Bid· them their privileges know;
Bid them with love of country glow;
With fkill, their arms defenfive wield,   505
Nor fhun the duties of the field."

" How blefs'd this heaven-diftinguifh'd land!
Where fchools in every hamlet ftand;
Far fpread the beams of learning bright,
And every child enjoys the light.   510
At fchool, beneath a faithful guide,
In teaching fkill'd, of morals tried,
And pleas'd the early mind to charm
To every good, from every harm,
Learn they to read, to write, to fpell,   515
And caft accompts, and learn them well:
For, on this microfcopic plan,
Is form'd the wife, and ufeful man.
Let him a tafte for books infpire;
While you, to nurfe the young defire,   520
A focial library procure,
And open knowledge to the poor.
This ufeful tafte imbib'd, your eyes
Shall fee a thoufand bleffings rife.
From haunts, and comrades vile fecure,   525
Where gilded baits to vice allure,
No more your fons abroad fhall roam,
But pleas'd, their evenings fpend at home;
Allurements more engaging find,
And feaft, with pure delight, the mind.   530
The realms of earth, their tho'ts fhall fcan,
And learn the works, and ways, of man;

See, from the favage, to the fage,
How nations ripen, age by age;
How ftates, and men, by virtue rife;   535
How both to ruin fink, by vice;
How thro' the world's great prifon-bounds,
While one wide clank of chains refounds,
Men flaves, while Angels weep to fee,
Some wife, and brave, and blefs'd, are free.   540
Thro' moral fcenes fhall ftretch their fight;
Difcern the bounds of wrong, and right;
That lothe; this love; and, pleas'd, purfue
Whate'er from man to man is due;
And, from the page of HEAVEN derive   546
The motives, and the means, to live."

" Nor think the fcope, or tafk, too great;
Coolly your leifure moments ftate;
Thefe, nicely reckon'd, will appear
Enough for all, that's promis'd here.   550
Would you ftill higher proof behold?
Plain facts that higher proof unfold.
I know, and tell it with a fmile,
No narrow lift of men of toil,
Illum'd by no collegiate rays,   555
And forc'd to tread in bufy ways,
Who yet, to read intenfely loving,
And every leifure hour improving,
On wifdom's heights diftinguifh'd ftand,
The boaft, and blefling, of our land.   560
This myftery learn: in great, or fmall things,
'TIS APPLICATION MASTERS ALL THINGS."

" *Thus taught, in every ftate of life,*
Of child, of parent, hufband, wife,
They'll wifer, better, happier, prove;   565
Their freedom better know, and love;

More pleasures gain, more hearts engage,
And feast their own dull hours of age."

" *Use them, and early use, to have,*
To earn, and what they earn, to save.   570
From industry, and prudence, flow
Relief of want, and balm of woe,
Delightful sleep, enduring wealth,
The purest peace, the firmest health,
True independence of our peers,   575
Support for sickness, and for years,
Security from household strife,
The conscience sweet of useful life,
Esteem abroad, content at home,
An easy passage to the tomb,   580
With blessings numberless, that flow
To neighbour, stranger, friend, and foe,
That man to man resistless bind,
And spread, and spread, to all mankind."

Would you for them this good acquire,   585
Prudence, and industry, inspire;
To habit bid the blessings grow;
Habits alone yield good below.
To these untrain'd, whate'er you give,
Whate'er inheritance you leave,   590
To every worthless passion given,
And scatter'd to the winds of heaven,
Will foes, and strangers, clothe, and feed;
While your own children pine with need,
Their friends, pain'd, pitied, slighted, fly, 595
Forgotten live, and wretched die.

" *In this New World, life's changing round,*
In three descents, is often found.
The *first*, firm, busy, plodding, poor,
Earns, saves, and daily swells, his store :   600

By farthings firſt, and pence, it grows;
In ſhillings next, and pounds, it flows;
Then ſpread his widening farms, abroad;
His foreſts wave; his harveſts nod;
Fattening, his numerous cattle play,   605
And debtors dread his reckoning day.
Ambitious then t'adorn with knowledge
His ſon, he places him at college;
And ſends, in ſmart attire, and neat,
To travel, thro' each neighbouring ſtate;   610
Builds him a handſome houſe, or buys,
Sees him a gentleman, and dies."

" The _ſecond_, born to wealth, and eaſe,
And taught to think, converſe, and pleaſe,
Ambitious, with his lady-wife,   615
Aims at a higher walk of life
Yet, in thoſe wholeſome habits train'd,
By which his wealth, and weight, were gain'd,
Bids care in hand with pleaſure go,
And blends œconomy with ſhow.   620
His houſes, fences, garden, dreſs,
The neat and thrifty man confeſs.
Improv'd, but with improvement plain,
Intent on office, as on gain,
Exploring, uſeful ſweets to ſpy,   625
To public life he turns his eye.
A townſman firſt; a juſtice ſoon;
A member of the houſe anon;
Perhaps to board, or bench, invited,
He ſees the ſtate, and ſubjects, righted;   630
And, raptur'd with politic life,
Conſigns his children to his wife.
Of houſhold cares amid the round,
For her, too hard the taſk is found.
At firſt ſhe ſtruggles, and contends;   635
Then doubts, deſponds, laments, and bends;

Her fons purfue the fad defeat,
And fhout their victory complete ;
Rejoicing, fee their father roam,
And riot, rake, and reign, at home.　　　　640
Too late he fees, and fees to mourn,
His race of every hope forlorn,
Abroad, for comfort, turns his eyes,
Bewails his dire miftakes, and dies."

　" His *heir, train'd only to enjoy,*　　　　645
Untaught his mind, or hands, t' employ,
Confcious of wealth enough for life,
With bufinefs, care, and worth, at ftrife,
By prudence, confcience, unreftrain'd,
And none, but pleafure's habits, gain'd,　　　　650
Whirls on the wild career of fenfe,
Nor danger marks, nor heeds expenfe.
Soon ended is the giddy round ;
And foon the fatal goal is found.
His lands, fecur'd for borrow'd gold,　　　　655
His houfes, horfes, herds, are fold.
And now, no more for wealth refpected,
He finks, by all his friends neglected ;
Friends, who, before, his vices flatter'd,
And liv'd upon the loaves he fcatter'd.　　　　660
Unacted every worthy part,
And pining with a broken heart,
To dirtieft company he flies,
Whores, gambles, turns a fot, and dies.
His children, born to fairer doom,　　　　665
In rags, purfue him to the tomb."

　" Apprentic'd then to mafters ftern,
Some real good the orphans learn ;
Are bred to toil, and hardy fare,
And grow to ufefulnefs, and care ;　　　　670
And, following their great-grandfire's plan,
Each flow becomes a ufeful man."

Pain'd, at each ftep, he fears himfelf undone,
And each new movement lofes all he won.
Thus fhall my fons their fhelter'd regions fave,
Firm as their hills, and as their fathers brave,
On freedom's force, with generous truft, rely,   335
And afk no fortrefs, but the favouring SKY."

    " Warm'd by that living fire, which HEAVEN beftows ;·
Which Freedom lights, and Independence blows ;
By that bright pomp, which moral fcenes difplay,
The unrivall'd grandeur of elective fway ;   340
And manners, where effulgent nature fhines,
Nor tinfel glares, nor faihion falfe refines,
At this beft æra, when, with glory bright,
Full-rifing Science cafts unclouded light,
Up wifdom's heights the foul fhall wing her way,   345
And climb thro' realms of ftill improving day."

    " Here wealth, from private mifery wrench'd no more,
To grace proud pomp, and fwell a monarch's ftore,
Aid venal hofts to blaft man's little joy,
And bid fell navies towns and realms deftroy,   350
For public blifs, from public hands, fhall flow,
And patriot works from patriot feelings grow.
See Appian ways acrofs the New World run !
Here hail the rifing, there the fetting, fun :
See long canals on earth's great convex bend !   355
Join unknown realms, and diftant oceans blend ;
In the Calm Main, Atlantic tides arife,
And Hudfon wanton under torrid fkies.
O'er all my climes, fee palac'd Science fmile !
And fchools unnumber'd gem the golden foil ;   360
For want, for woe, the neat afylum rife,
And countlefs temples call propitious fkies.
By locks immenfe fee broken rivers join'd ;
And the vaft bridge my Rhines, and Danubes, bind ;

For ufeful fabrics, fpacious domes afcend ;   365
Huge engines roll, and ftreams their currents bend."

  " Here too, each heart, alive to pity's caufe,
Shall curfe ftill-favage Europe's reeking laws ;
That gibbets plant, as erft the foreft ftood ;
With horfe-leach thirft, cry, "Give us daily blood ;" 370
Void, not of mercy, but of common fenfe,
Commute a human life for thirteen pence ;
Poor debtors chain, to glut revenge and pride,
And one man hang, that other men may ride."

  " Here firft, fince earth beneath the deluge ftood, 375
Bloodfhed alone fhall be aton'd by blood :
All other crimes, unfit with man to dwell,
The wretch fhall expiate, in the lonely cell :
There awful Confcience, and an anguifh'd heart,
Shall ftretch the rack, and wing the flaming dart ; 380
Approaching fiends with lowering vengeance glow,
And gulphs yawn downward to the world of woe.
Half feen, at times, and trembling faint, from far,
Shall dawn fwcet Mercy's bright and beamy ftar ;
Hope enter, fmite his chains, and fet him free, 385
And fpread her wings, and whifper, " Follow me."
In this dread manfion, fhall the culprit find
His country's laws, not juft alone, but kind ;
And fed, and clad, and lodg'd, with comfort, feel
Whatever good deftroys not public weal." 390

  " Here too, her fcope fhall Policy extend,
Nor to check crimes be ftill her fingle end.
Her hand fhall aid the poor, the fad confole,
And lift up merit from it's lowly ftool,
Reach to th' induftrious youth the means to thrive, 395
The orphan fhelter, bid the widow live,
Nurfe, with a foftering care, each art refin'd,
That mends the manners, or that lights the mind,

The choking damps of foul defpair expel,
And help afpiring genius to excel." 400

" See, in each village, treafur'd volumes ftand !
And fpread pure knowledge through th' enlighten'd land ;
Knowledge, the wife Republic's ftanding force,
Subjecting all things, with refiftlefs courfe ;
That bids the ruler hold a righteous fway, 405
And bends perfuaded freemen to obey.
Frequent, behold the rich Mufeum yield
The wonders dread of Nature's fruitful field !
See ftrong invention engines ftrange devife,
And ope the myfteries of earth, feas, and fkies ; 410
Aid curious art to finifh works refin'd,
And teach abftrufeft fcience to mankind."

" Up the dread vault, where ftars immenfely roll,
To heaven, Herfchelian tubes conduct the foul ;
Where proud Orion heads th' immortal train, 415
And opes his lucid window through the main ;
Where, far beyond this limitary fky,
Superior worlds of liquid fplendour lie ;
Far other funs diffufe th' unfetting ray,
And other planets roll, in living day, 420
Truth, blifs, and virtue, age by age, refine,
And unknown nations bafk in life divine,"

" Even now fair beams around my concave burn,
The golden Phofphor of th' expanding morn.
See raptur'd Franklin, when fierce tempefts ride, 425
Down the fafe dome innoxious lightnings guide !
The nice machine fee felf-taught Kingfley frame,
That, unexampled, pours th' electric flame !
See Rittenhoufe, and Pope, with art their own,
Roll the fmall fyftem round the mimic fun ! 430
See Bufhnell's ftrong, creative genius, fraught
With all th' affembled powers of fkilful thought,

U

His myftic veffel plunge beneath the waves,
And glide thro' dark retreats, and coral caves!
While crowds, around them, join the glorious ftrife, 435
And eafe the load, that lies on human life."

" Nor lefs their ftrength fhall private efforts blend,
My fons t' illume, refine, exalt, amend.
Thro' Nature's field fhall bold Inquiry ftray,
Where Europe's Genius leads the fplendid way; 440
Tell why the winds with fickle wanderings blow,
Thin vapours fpring, and clouds condenfing flow ;
From what ftrange caufe th' etherial phafes rife,
And gloom, and glory, change fo foon the fkies ;
How heat through nature fpreads its chemic power ; 445
Wakes the foft fpring, diffolves the icy fhower,
In fluid fplendour bids the metal glow,
Commands the ftream to roll, the flower to blow,
With golden beauty lights the ftarry choir,
And warms th' exhauftlefs fun with living fire. 450
Or pierce the mift of elemental ftrife,
See lazy matter roufing into life ;
It's parts meet, mix, repel, attract, combine,
And mould the plant with infinite defign ;
Or through the grades of nobler life afcend, 455
And the ftrange, acting, fuffering Being blend ;
Or ceafe their hold, to bring new forms to light,
And bid the fairy ftructure melt from fight ;
Or round the globe it's wondrous ftrata fpread,
Fafhion the hills, and vault the ocean's bed ; 460
Imblaze the ore, th' enticing gem unfold,
And with pure funbeams tinge the lafting gold.
Here too fhall Genius learn, by what controul,
Th' inftinctive magnet trembles to the pole ;
With curious eye, it's fyftem'd errors trace, 465
And teach the myftic longitude of place :
Or through the bright, Columbian fcience rove,
Purfue the lightning's path, in realms above,

Or o'er earth's bowels, mark it's silent courfe,
And fee all nature own it's magic force :   470
Or ope more awful wonders to mankind,
Evolve the terrors of the Indian wind,
Tell whence volcanic fires the mount inform,
Whence heave the plains, or burfts the raging ftorm;
Whence the wide concave angry meteors rend,   475
And fhuddering earth quakes to it's diftant end :
Or, in dark paths, where health's fair ftreamlets ftray,
Thro' plants, and mines, explore their chemic way,
Redrefs the ravage of encroaching clime,
Change the fad curfe, rebuild the wafte of time,   480
Protract man's date, bid age with verdure bloom,
And ftrew with flowers the journey to the tomb."

" See rifing bards afcend the fteep of fame !
Where truth commends, and virtue gives a name,
With Homer's life, with Milton's ftrength, afpire,   485
Or catch divine Ifaiah's hallow'd fire.
No fickly fpot fhall foil the page refin'd ;
Lend vice a charm, or taint the artlefs mind ;
Another Pope inchanting themes rehearfe,
Nor the meek virgin blufh to hear the verfe ;   490
Improv'd, and clouded with no courtly ftain,
A whiter page than Addifon's remain."

" On the bright canvas, fee the pencil trace
Unrivall'd forms of glory, and of grace !
In the fair field, no traits of vilenefs fpring,   495
No wanton lordling, and no bloody king,
No ftrumpet, handed to perpetual fame,
No fcenes of lewdnefs, and no deeds of fhame :
But men, that counfell'd, fought, and bled, for men,
And held, to death, the world-renewing pen ;   500
Scenes, that would Envy of her fnakes beguile,
Deeds, where fond Virtue loves to gaze, and fmile :

Such forms, fuch deeds, on Raphael's tablets fhine,
And fuch, O Trumbull! glow alike on thine."

"No more fhall Mufic trill, with raptures, o'er   505
The fwinifh revel, and the lewd amour,'
The phrenzied ravage of the blood-ftain'd car,
Or the low triumphs of the Sylvan war.
But Sorrow's filent fadnefs fweetly charm,
With love infpire, with real glory warm,   510
Wake, in Religion's caufe, diviner lays,
And fill the bofom with Messiah's praife."

"But chief, my fons fhall Moral fcience trace,
Man's nature, duties, dignity, and place;
How, in each clafs, the nice relation fprings,   515
To God, to man, to fubjects, and to kings;
How tafte, myfterious, in the Heavenly plan,
Improves, adorns, and elevates, the man;
How balanc'd powers, in juft gradation, prove
The means of order, freedom, peace, and love,   520
Of blifs, at home, of homage fair, abroad,
Juftice to man, and piety to God."

"For foon, no more to philofophic whims,
To cloud-built theories, and lunar dreams,
But to firm facts, fhall human faith be given,   525
The proofs of Reafon, and the voice of Heaven.
No more by light Voltaire with bubbles fed,
With Hume's vile hufks no longer mock'd for bread,
No more by St. John's lantern lur'd aftray,
Through moors, and mazes, from the broad highway,   530
Tranfported men the path of life fhall know,
And Angels' food fhower round them, as they go."

"The Word of life, a world of ftores refin'd,
The drefs, the feaft, the riches, of the mind,
The bold Divine, commercing, fhall explore,   535
Search every realm, and vifit every fhore,

Thence wines, and fruits, of every tafte, and clime,
Matur'd, and beauteous, in immortal prime,
Thence gems collect, and gold from wifdom's mine,
Robes of pure white, and ornaments divine,   540
(Whate'er can bid the famifh'd wretch refpire,
Or clothe the naked in unftain'd attire)
To HEAVEN's high altar bring the offering blefs'd,
And all mankind, his Levites, fhare the feaft."

    For here, alike to want, and wealth, allied,   545
Plac'd in the mean, 'twixt poverty and pride,
The goal, where faithful virtue moft is found,
The goal, where ftrong temptations leaft abound,
Nor floth benumbs, nor luxury betrays,
Nor fplendour awes, nor lures to dangerous ways,   550
Where the poor boldly tell their woes fevere,
Fear no neglect, and find the mingling tear,
From civil toils, cabals, and party-heat,
My facred clerks fpontaneous fhall retreat;
To others leave to others what is given,   555
And fhine, the mere ambaffadors of HEAVEN;
Spread truth, build virtue, forrow foothe, and pain,
And rear primæval piety again."

    " The nobleft Manners too my realms fhall cheer,
With prudence, frank; obliging, yet fincere;   560
Great, without pride; familiar, yet refin'd;
The honeft face difclofing all the mind;
Stanhope abjur'd; the Gofpel own'd alone;
And all, from other's claim'd, to others done.
Here nature's fweet fimplicity fhall reign,   565
And art's foul tincture meet a juft difdain;
The waxen mien of Europe's courtly lords;
Love fpent in looks, and honour loft in words;
Where fad ambition, fickening, toils for fhow,
And fmiles, invented, mafk the face of woe;   570

Where life drags on, a difappointing round,
Where hope's a cheat, and happinefs a found."

" What though, like Europe's titled train to live,
Even in thefe climes, the fplendid trifler ftrive;
Pine, with a fickly appetite, for fhew,   575
And, every year, the income fpend of two;
With aukward folly, mimic toilfome fin,
Parade without, and wretchednefs within;
Yet faint, and few, fhall thefe corruptions fpread,
Seen but to be defpis'd, and hifs'd, and fled.   580
Strong fenfe fhall here the life of reafon yield,
Each whim exploded, and each vice expell'd;
From fweet affections actions fweet fhall flow,
All that makes joy, and all that quiets woe,
Where nature, friendfhip, love, unrivall'd reign,   585
And form anew the dignity of men."

" And O what beams fhall light the Fair-one's mind!
How the foft eye-ball gliften truth refin'd!
What featur'd harmony mild virtue form!
With what fweet fympathy, the bofom warm!   590
To wifdom pure, by ufeful fcience train'd,
From fafhions, cards, and plays, to reafon gain'd,
To fhow, to flattery, victims now no more,
Vile forms extinct, and idle follies o'er,
Anew to duty fhall the heart be given,   595
Love to mankind, and piety to HEAVEN.
Grac'd with each beauty of th' etherial form,
Led by a heart, with rich affections warm,
Each lovely daughter, fifter, friend, and wife,
Shall call forth rofes, from the thorns of life;   600
With foothing tendernefs, rough man refine,
Wake gentler thoughts, and prompt to deeds divine;
Through wifdom's paths, their tender offspring charm,
And bear them upward, with fupporting arm;

Plant truth's fair feeds ; the budding virtues tend ;   650
And bid the nurfling faint a cherub end.
Like vernal dews, .their kindnefs fhall diftil,
Cheer the fad foul, and lighten every ill ;
Breathe balmy comfort round the wretches fhed,
And lay the outcaft in a peaceful bed ;   610
Bid, round their manfions, blifs domeftic rife,
And fix a bright refemblance of the fkies."

  " Through this wide world, outfpread from fky to fky,
Thus envied fcenes of rapture meet the eye.
Then, on the borders of this fapphire plain,   615
Shall growing beauties grace my fair domain.
O'er thefe green hills, and in each fmiling dell,
Where elves might haunt, and fays delighted dwell,
From Thames's walks, to Hudfon's verdant ifles,
See, with fair feats, my lovely margin fmiles !   620
No domes of pomp infult the fmiling plain ;
Nor lords, nor princes, trample freeborn man.
Man, the firft title known beneath the fkies ;
A prince, when virtuous, and a lord, when wife.
See, circling each, with fimple luftre, fpread   625
The neat inclofure, and the happy fhade ;
Meads green with fpring ; with Autumn orchards fair ;
And fields, where culture bids all climes appear ,
Gay groves exult ; Chinefian gardens glow,
And bright reflections paint the wave below !"   630

  " On this blue plain, my eye fhall then behold
Earth's diftant realms immingled fails unfold ;
Proud Europe's towers, her thunders laid afleep,
Float, in calm filence, o'er th' aftonifh'd deep ;
Peru unfetter'd lift her golden fails,   635
And filken India waft on fpicy gales ;
From death's dull fhade, awaken'd Afric rife,
And roll the products of her funny fkies.

Here fhall they learn what manners blifs affure ;
What fway creates it, and what laws fecure,   640
See pride abas'd ; the wolfifh heart refin'd ;
Th' unfetter'd confcience, and th' unpinion'd mind ;
To human good all human efforts given ;
Nor war infult, nor bondage anger, HEAVEN ;
No favage courfe of Eaftern glory run ;   645
Atchiev'd no conqueft, and no realm undone."

" Here fhall they fee an æra new of Fame,
Where fcience wreathes, and worth confers a name ;
No more her temple ftand in human gore ;
Of human bones, her columns rife no more :   750
The life, by poets fung, the heavens approve,
Wifdom commend, and future ages love."

" From yon blue wave, to that far diftant fhore,
Where funs decline, and evening oceans roar,
Their eyes fhall view one free elective fway;   655
One blood, one kindred, reach from fea to fea ;
One language fpread ; one tide of manners run ;
One fcheme of fcience, and of morals one ;
And, GOD's own Word the ftructure, and the bafe,
One faith extend, one worfhip, and one praife."   660

" Thefe fhall they fee, amaz'd ; and thefe convey,
On rapture's pinions, o'er the diftant fea ;
New light, new glory, fire the general mind,
And peace, and freedom, re-illume mankind."

END OF THE SEVENTH PART.

NOTES to PART I.

LINE 42. The parish of Greenfield confifts of about thirteen fquare miles. On this little tract were found, at the time of the late cenfus, almoft fourteen hundred inhabitants: a population as great, as that of Britain, if the accounts which I have feen, of the extent and population of that country, are juft. The people of Greenfield are almoft all Farmers, and have no advantages for fupport, befides thofe which are common to N. England in general. Thus without any peculiar affiftance from commerce, or manufacturing, an immenfe population can exift on the mere labours of the hufbandman. The people of Greenfield, alfo, very generally abound in the neceffaries and comforts of life. Such are the effects of an equal divifion of property, and of the cultivation of lands by the proprietors.

L. 85. No country has been more unjuftly or contemptibly flandered, than New England.

L. 94. [Firms.] I have ventured to ufe this word, as a verb. It appeared to me better to exprefs the idea intended, than any other word, which I could recollect.

L. 177. A remarkable proof of the mildnefs of manners, in New England, exifted during the late war. The inhabitants were at leaft as much divided, and as directly oppofed, both in opinion and conduct, as thofe of France; and through a much longer period. (a) Yet not one perfon was put to death by the hand of violence, and but one by the hand of civil juftice, during an eight years war, and in a country containing a million of inhabitants.

L. 215. The State of Connecticut exhibits the moft uniform and unmixed manners, to be found in New England; and thofe, which may, with the greateft propriety, be called the national manners of that country.

L. 223. The happinefs of the inhabitants of Connecticut appears, like their manners, morals, and government, to exceed any thing, of which the Eaftern continent could ever boaft. A thorough and impartial developement of the ftate of fociety, in Connecticut, and a complete inveftigation of the fources of its happinefs, would probably throw more light on the true methods of promoting the interefts of mankind, than all the volumes of philofophy, which have been written. The caufes, which have already produced happinefs, will ever produce it. To facts alone, there-

(a) *January* 1, 1793.

X

fore, ought we to refort, if we would obtain this important knowledge. Theories are ufually mere dreams; fitted to amufe, not to inftruct; and Philofophers, at leaft political ones, are ufually mere Theorifts. The common fenfe of the early Colonifts of New England faw farther into political fubjects, thofe at leaft, which are of great importance to hu man happinefs, than all tne Phil fophers, who have written fince the world began.

L. 225. Nothing can be more vifionary, than many modern Philofophic opinions, con erning gover ment. All human fyftems, refpecting practical fubjects, unlefs derived from facts, will ever be vifionary, and deferve to be clased with fubftantial forms, fubtil matter, and atomic tendency to exertion. Man is wholly unable, by mere contemplation, to bring into his view a number of principles fufficient to conftitute a theory, which can confift with practice. One would imagine, hat the univerfal fate of hyp thetical philofophy muft long fince have taught ingenious men this obvious truth; but the pleafure of making, and defending, fyftems, is fo great, that fuch men are ftill employed in building air-caftles, and in ferioufly expecting to inhabit them.

L. 234. If gentlemen, w o are natives of Europe, fhould think this paragraph harfh, or unfounded, the writer requefts them fo far to turn th ir attention to the feveral facts, mentioned in it, as to fatisfy themfelves, whether the afcription be juft, or erroneous. The natives of Great Britain, particularly, will find, in diftinguifhed writers of that country, defcriptions of Britifh fociety, warranting all, that is afferted in this poem: defcriptions confirmed, fo far, at leaft, as the author's acquaintance has extended, by thofe Americans, who have travelled into Britain. The *Tafk*, one of the moft fenfible and valuable performances, in the ·Englifh language, is alone a fufficient juftification of no fmall part of what is here declared.

L. 247. It is, perhaps, not to be wondered at, that the ftate of fociety, lately exifting in France, fhould be followed by extenfive and ridiculous infidelity; but that fuch a fpeech as that faid to be uttered, Dec. 1792, by Citizen Dupont, fhould have been fpoken by any man, on any occafion, and before any audience, would hardly have been believed, unlefs pub ifhed with high authe tication. That it fhould have been uttered by a man, characterized as a man of weight and influence, is ftill more aftonifhing: and that it fhould have been received, by the Legiflative Affembly of a great Nation, with applaufe, is a fact, which, if it fhould, unhappily for the honour of human nature, be handed to pofterity, will probably be regarded rather as a Provencal legend, than as a reality. Of the like contemptible character are the later declarations of Citizen Lacroix, on the petition of the Quakers and Anabaptifts; in which are the following words. " The Conftitution is my Gofpel, and Liberty is my God. I know no other." Thefe gentlemen appear ambitious of rivalling the character of Aretine, on whofe tomb this infcription is faid to have been written.

Here lies Aretine,
Who fpoke evil of every one,
But h s God;
And in this he muft be excufed,
Becaufe he did not know him.

L. 248. I have feen a memorial, faid to be prefented to his Britifh Majefty, by the Lord Mayor, Aldermen, and Common Council, of London;

in which they declare, that within ten years, 4,800 perfons had, in that city, been convicted of felony. (a) In New England, which contains more inhabitants than London, it is to be queftioned, whether, in any ten years, fince it was fettled by the Englifh, there have been ten perfons convicted of felony. A partial account, for this enormous difproportion, may be found in the mildnefs of the laws of New England, which are far lefs fanguinary, than thofe of Great Britain. It may alfo be juftly obferved, that London is a city of enormous wealth, and enormous poverty, and a general receptacle of fharpers and villains from the whole Britifh empire; as well as from feveral other countries. But it is alfo to be remembered, that a great proportion of the felons, convicted in New England, are natives of Europe. It is probable, that the fubject cannot be explained in any manner, which will not involve, as its principal caufes, the very great difference, in the refpective places, to be found in the univerfality of happinefs, and in the purity of morals.

L. 267. [See every heart, &c.] The fafhions of Europe, efpecially of Britain and France, fuit neither the climate, the convenience, the policy, the property, nor the character, of this country. The changes of climate in this country require modes of dreffing very different from thofe, which are healthful in France and England. The Americans are generally people of bufinefs, and, of courfe, muft be greatly and con inual y incommoded by an adoption of many foreign fafhions. Our policy naturally teaches us to reject all fervile imitation of the manners of other countries; and all conftant imitation is attended with fervility. The dignified character of free republicans ought to lead them to defpife a perpetual change in the figure of drefs; to aim only at fuch modes as are convenient, and to perfevere in them; to fhew their independ nce, in the choice of their own modes, and their ingenuity in the invention of them; and to manifeft a total fuperiority to the miferable frippery of artificial fociety. In the mean time, our pecuniary circumftances would be advantageoufly confulted, by the adoption of drefs, in all refpects fuch as might well confift with our general mediocrity of wealth. The Friends appear to fhew much good fenfe on this fubject.

L. 279. War has exifted, in fome, or other, of the countries of Europe, 75 years, out of the 92, which have elapfed, fince the beginning of the prefent century; a century boafted of, as the moft enlightened, refined, and humane, within the knowledge of mankind. The caufes of thefe wars have, alfo, been generally fuch, as ought to cover the authors of them with deep and perpetual infamy.

L. 296. Few objects more demand the attention of men of influence, in this country, than 'the eftablifhment of national manners. That much may be done, for this purpofe, will not, I prefume, be queftioned, There are but two, or three countries, in the United States, in which the manners have any thing like a general uniformity: the low country of Virginia, the low country of South Carolina, and New England. The manners of Virginia and South Carolina cannot be eafily continued, without the continuance of the Negro flavery; an event, which can fcarcely be expected. The manners of New England appear to be rapidly fpreading through the American republic; the natives of that country being generally

---

(a) *In the Lent circuit* (1786) 286 *perfons were capitally convicted in England; and from* 960 *to* 1000 *convicts are now annually tranfported from that country.*

even more tenacious of their manners, when abroad, than when at home. When the enterprize, induſtry, œconomy, morals, and happineſs, of New England, eſpecially of Connecticut, are attentively conſidered, the patriotic mind will perhaps find much more reaſon to rejoice in this proſpect, than to regret it.

L. 297. [Think whence this weal aroſe.] The peculiar proſperity of New England in general, and particularly of Maſſachuſetts and Connecticut, undoubtedly ariſes from the equal diviſion of property, the univerſal eſtabliſhment of ſchools, and their peculiar manner of ſupporting the goſpel.

L. 430. [Ah! knew he but his happineſs, &c.] Ah! knew he but his happineſs, of men the happieſt he, &c. *Thomſon.*

O fortunatos nimium, ſua ſi bona norint,
Agricolas! *Virgil Georg.* 2.

L. 573. Dan. 12. 13.

N O T E S TO P A R T II.

LINE 1. This part of the poem, though appropriated to the pariſh of Greenfield, may be conſidered as a general deſcription of the towns and villages of New England ; thoſe only excepted, which are either commercial, new, or ſituated on a barren ſoil. Moroſe and gloomy perſons, and perhaps ſome others, may think the deſcription too highly coloured. Perſons of moderation and candour may poſſibly think otherwiſe. In its full extent, the writer ſuppoſes it applicable to the beſt inhabitants only ; but he believes the number of theſe to be great: to others he thinks it partially applicable. Poetical repreſentations are uſually eſteemed flattering; poſſibly this is as little ſo, as moſt of them. The inhabitants of New England, notwithſtanding ſome modern inſtances of declenſion, are, at leaſt in the Writer's opinion, a ſingular example of virtue and happineſs.

It will be eaſily diſcovered by the reader, that this part of the poem is deſigned to illuſtrate the effects of the ſtate of property, which is the counter part to that, ſo beautifully exhibited by Dr. Goldſmith, in the Deſerted Village. That excellent writer, in a moſt intereſting manner, diſplays the wretched condition of the many, where enormous wealth, ſplendour, and luxury, conſtitute the ſtate of the few. In this imperfect attempt, the writer wiſhed to exhibit the bleſſings, which flow from an equal diviſion of property, and a general competence.

Wherever an *equal diviſion of property* is mentioned, in this Work, the Reader is requeſted to remember, that that ſtate of things only is intended, in which every citizen is ſecured in the avails of his induſtry and prudence, and in which property deſcends, by law, in equal ſhares, to the proprietor's children.

L. 1. Sweet Auburn, lovelieſt village of the plain! *Goldſmith.*

L. 12. [The ſpring bird.] A ſmall bird, called, in ſome parts of New England, by that name; which appears, very early in the ſpring, on the banks of brooks and ſmall rivers, and ſings a very ſweet and ſprightly note.

(4) L. 26. [Slump'd.] This word, ſaid, in England, to be of North Country original, is cuſtomarily uſed in New England, to denote the ſudden ſinking of the ſoot in the earth, when partially thawn, as in the month of March. It is alſo uſed to denote the ſudden ſinking of the earth under the ſoot.

L. 28. [Nutwood.] Hickory.

L. 45. And, many a year elapſed, return'd to view.

⋅ *Goldſmith.*

L. 49. Yes, let the rich deride, the proud diſdain. *Goldſmith.*

L. 52. — — — — — The gloſs of art.

Goldſmith.

L. 68. And parting ſummer's lingring blooms delayed.

L. 73. Sweet-ſmiling village! lovelieſt of the lawn. *Goldſmith.*

Goldſmith.

L. 75. In ſeveral parts of this country, the roads through villages are called ſtreets.

L. 79, and 80. And every want, to opulence allied,
And every pang that folly pays to pride. *Goldſmith.*

L. 91, O luxury! thou curſt by heaven's decree. *Goldſmith.*

L. 91, &c. Men in middling circumſtances appear greatly to excel the rich, in piety, charity, and public ſpirit; nor will a critical obſerver of human life heſitate to believe, that they enjoy more happineſs.

L. 145. [Farmer.] Farmer of revenue: A ſuperior kind of tax-gatherer, in ſome countries of Europe.

L. 154. By poverty's unconquerable bar. *Beattie.*

L. 196. [Wain.] Waggon, or cart.

L. 208. Some intereſting and reſpeetable efforts have been made, in Connecticut, and others are now making, for the purpoſe of freeing the Negroes.

L. 221. The black children are generally ſprightly and ingenious, until they become conſcious of their ſlavery. This uſually happens, when they are 4, 5, or 6 years of age. From that time, they uſually ſink into ſtupidity, or give themſelves up to vice.

L. 237. If we conſider how few inducements the blacks have to ingenious, or worthy efforts, we ſhall more wonder, that there are, among them, ſo many, than that there are ſo few, examples of ingenuity or amiableneſs.

L. 244. [Eſſoins.] Excuſes.

L. 251, 252. [Home, Monboddo.] Two modern philoſophers, who have publiſhed ſeveral ingenious dreams, concerning the firſt inhabitants of this world.

L. 285, &c. The facts, alleged in this paragraph, are ſo generally known, as not to need particular proof.

L. 295. See the ſpeech of Mr. Briſſot, in the National Aſſembly of France, Dec. 1, 1791. If the authority here quoted, for theſe particular inſtances of cruelty, exerciſed on the unhappy Africans, in the Weſt Indies, ſhould be thought doubtful, the reader may find, in the evidence taken, on this ſubject, by the Committee of the Britiſh Houſe of Commons, an immenſe number of inſtances, in which inhumanity, equally reprehenſible, has been undoubtedly practiſed on theſe unhappy people.

L. 301. Of this fact, I was informed by a gentleman of reputation, who affured me that he had fufficient evidence of its reality.

L. 305. In fome of the Weft India Iflands, it is a cuftom, to fend, on Monday morning efpecially, offending flaves to the docks; each carrying a billet, declaring the tranfgreffion, and the number of ftripes the offender is to receive, and containing a piftareen to pay for the infliction of them.— There the offenders are raifed up, fucceffively, by a crane, and ftretched by heavy weights, appended to their ancles In this pofture, they are moft cruelly tortured by the cowfkin, and ftill more cruelly, it is faid, by a briar, called ebony; which is ufed to let out the blood, where it has been ftarted by the whip.

L. 368. The Academical fchool, mentioned in the preface.

L. 473, 474. No more thy glaffy brook reflects the day :
But, choked with fedges, works it's weedy way:
Goldfmith.

L. 476. The red-breaft of America is a remarkably fweet finger.

L. 478. The houfe, here referred to, ftands at fome diftance from the road.

L. 524. Prov. 31. 11.

L. 532. Prov. 31. 28.

L. 538. Deut. 24. 15.

L. 552. Mrs. Eleanor Sherwood, the excellent perfon, whofe character has been given above, died of the fmall pox, March 29, 1793; fometime after this character was given.

L. 589. Pier. A looking glafs; from it's place, and afterwards from a particular ftructure, called a pier-glafs.

Ibid. All perfons declare formal vifiting to be unpleafing and burthenfome, and familiar vifiting to be pleafing; yet multitudes fpend no fmall part of their lives, in formal vifiting, and confider themfelves as being under a fpecies of obligation to it. In formal vifiting, perfons go to be feen; in focial vifiting, to give and to receive, pleafure. If common fenfe were allowed to dictate, or genuine good breeding to influence, we fhould immediately exchange form and parade, for fociality and happinefs.

L. 617. I do not remember ever to have feen a lady, in full drefs, who appeared to be fo happy, or to behave fo eafily, and gracefully, as when fhe was moderately dreffed. An unufual degree of drefs feems uniformly to infpire formality, diftance, and difficulty of behaviour. Toil, tafte, and fancy, are put to exertion, to contrive, and to adjuft, the drefs, which is expected highly to ornament the perfon; and the fame exertion, appears to be ufed in contriving, and fafhioning, manners, which may become the drefs.

L. 712. [Afian fea.] Pacific ocean.

L. 720. [Korean.] Korea is a large peninfula on the eaftern fhore of Afia.

L. 731. [Albion.] New Albion; a very defirable country, on the weftern fhore of America, difcovered by Sir Francis Drake.

L. 735. [Mexic hills.] A range of mountains, running from north to fouth, at the diftance of feveral hundred miles, weftward of the Miffifippi,

L. 736. [Louis.] The Miffifippi. [Sicilian fong.] Paftoral poetry.

NOTES to PART III.

LINE 15. On the plain, on which Fairfield is built, are several eminences of uncommon beauty.

L. 115. There were several acts of grofs abuse, and of savage barbarity, practised by the Britifh, when they burned Fairfield.

L. 143. That inferiors, in subordination, are bound to obey all, even the unjuft and immoral commands of their superiors, and that the inferior is, in this conduct, juftifiable, and the superior alone guilty, is ftill not un-'frequently afferted, and therefore probably believed. When it shall be right to do evil, that good may come, when crimes and virtuous actions, with the guilt, and the merit, of them shall become transferable, when man shall ceafe to be accountable to his MAKER, and when GOD shall no more rule, with rightful authority, over his own creatures, this doctrine will probably reft on a more folid bafis.

L. 181. None of the numerous and horrid evils of war is more wanton, more ufelefs, and more indicative of the worft character, than burning. No nation, by which it is either allowed, or done, ought to make a claim to humanity, or civilization.

L. 231. There was a heavy thunder ftorm, on the night, in which Fairfield was burned; yet fuch was the confufion and diftrefs of the remaining inhabitants, that feveral of them did not perceive it.

L. 168. From Fairfield, the Britifh proceeded to Norwalk; which they burned, the next day. It deferves to be remembered, that, during the conflagration. Governor Tryon had a chair carried to the top of an eminence, in that town, called Grummon's hill; and there, at his eafe, enjoyed the profpect, and the pleafure, of the fcene. Two churches, 135 dwelling houfes, with a proportional number of other buildings, were deftroyed, at Norwalk. Eight other towns, in the United States, experienced the fame fate; and while immenfe evil was done to the inhabitants, no benefit accrued, as none plainly could accrue, to their enemies.

L. 365. It is probable, that more of human labour, ingenuity, and property, has been expended in the various bufinefs of deftruction, than in all the arts, by which peace and happinefs have been promoted.

L. 405. Every perfon, acquainted with the hiftory of the Romans, knows that the temple of Janus was fhut, whenever they were in a ftate of peace, and that this happened but twice, during the firft 750 years of their national exiftence. Mankind in general have been engaged in war, with almoft as little intermiffion.

It would be worth the labour of fome friend to mankind, to prefent the public with a complete view of the time, during which war has exifted in Europe, fince the deftruction of the Roman empire; the number of nations concerned in each war; the fums expended; the debts incurred; the foldiers, failors, and citizens, deftroyed; the cities, towns, and villages, burnt, plundered, and ruined; the miferies, known to be fuffered; the moft probable caufes of the refpective wars; and the gain refulting to the refpective combatants. Thofe, who have accefs to large libraries, would probably find, in them, much of the information, neceffary to a defign of this nature.

L. 487. The injury, done by war, to the morals of a country, is inferior to none of the evils, which it suffers. A century is insufficient to repair the moral waste of a short war.

L. 553. [Go then, ah go.] It is probable, that whenever mankind shall cease to make war, this most desirable event will arise from the general opposition, made to war, by the common voice. Hence the peculiar importance of diffusing this opposition, as widely as possible, especially by education. If parents, school-masters, and clergymen, would unite their efforts, for this most benevolent and glorious purpose, the effects of such an union, on the rising generation, would probably exceed the most sanguine hopes.

L. 601. Some of the fixed stars are, from evident alterations in their appearance, called changeable stars. The star, Aegol, or Medusa's head, is a remarkable one; and changes, from the first, to the fourth magnitude.

L. 659. The custom of privateering is one of the reliques of Gothic barbarity. No good reason can be given, why commissions, to plunder and destroy houses, should not be given to private persons, as well as to plunder and destroy vessels; to rob on the land, as well as on the sea; and why such persons, as resisted, should not be put to death, in the one case, as well as in the other. Custom, it is presumed, is the only ground of any difference of opinion, with regard to the cases proposed. All privateering is robbery, and murder; and the government, which sanctions privateering, is guilty of authorizing these horrid crimes. Nor can the merchant, who is the proprietor, be excused from his share in the guilt.

NOTES TO PART IV.

LINE 8, 9. Rev. 18. 7.
L. 10, &c. Dan. 2, 31, &c. 37, &c.
L. 14. [Timur.] Tamerlane, a Samarcand Tartar; who, in a short time, conquered what is now called Turkey in Asia, Persia, and India; together with several parts of Russia, and Tartary: the whole being an extent of territory larger than the Roman empire.
L. 38. [Demon chiefs.] Demons, according to the opinions of the ancient heathens, were beings of a middle character, between gods and men. The souls of departed heroes were ranked in this class of beings.
L. 43. [Trident.] The fabled sceptre of Neptune, the heathen god of the sea.
L. 118. [Sere.] Furrowed, wrinkled.
L. 131. The heroism, exhibited by our ancestors, in their wars with the Indians, and the patriotism, generally displayed, in their public conduct, have scarcely been excelled.

L. 180. The Indians of this country appear generally to have worfhipped an evil dæmon, with a hope of averting his ill offices. This deity was however efteemed inferior to the Great or Good Spirit.

L. 186. Sacrifices of this nature are, at the prefent time, faid to be offered by the Senecas.

L. 190. The Pequods ufed a religious dance, accompanied with fongs, which they performed in a fmall circular fpot, refembling the circus of the ancient Romans.

L. 191. [Thyas.] The prieftefs of Bacchus. [Nyfa.] A city in India, faid to be built by Bacchus, in which his worfhip was efpecially celebrated.

L. 224. The Indians have generally fuppofed the future world of happinefs to lie in the weftern regions. The reafon feems to be the fame with that, which induces the Negroes to believe the happy world fituated in Africa; viz. that it was the country, whence they originated. A fimilar opinion appears to have exifted among feveral, perhaps moft, ignorant colonifts, for fome time, after their emigration.

L. 269. [Sheen.] Brightnefs.

L. 298. [Elliot, Mayhew.] Thefe excellent men have proved, beyond difpute, that the Indians may be civilized, and chriftianized, by proper efforts. Their Apoftolic piety ought to be remembered, with perpetual honour; and well deferves a public monument, from the State, of which they were ornaments, as well as citizens.

L. 307. The greateft obftacle to chriftianizing the Indians is now, as it has ufually been, their rivetted perfuafion, that the Britifh Colonifts, in all their correfpondence with them, have aimed at their own benefit, not at the benefit of the Indians; at the acquifition of their lands, not at the falvation of their fouls: a perfuafion founded on too unequivocal and fhameful proof. So long as thofe, who trade with them, are allowed to poifon them by all the means of corruption, virtuous men can only regret their miferable condition. It is to be hoped, that the late act of Congrefs, regulating our correfpondence with the Indians, together with feveral other humane and juft meafures of the fame nature, meafures which reflect the higheft honour on that Body, will, in a good degree, remove thefe evils.

L. 311. [India's curfe.] Rum.

L. 351. The French fettlers of Canada took unceafing and immenfe pains, to induce the Indians to quarrel with the Englifh Colonifts. To this conduct they were influenced not lefs by religious motives, than by thofe of policy, and by what has been called national enmity.

L. 362. The hill, to which the Pequods retired, has the appearance of being artificial.

L. 394. The heroifm, celebrated by Homer, Virgil, and other Greek and Latin Poets, principally confifted of feats of perfonal prowefs, and the conduct of fmall parties. Such was the gallantry of the firft American Colonifts.

Y

NOTES to PART V.

L. 21.   [Weſtern Albion.] N. England.
L. 79.   Moſes. See the book of Deuteronomy.
L. 80.   Joſhua. See Joſh. 23. 24.
L. 109.   Mat. 16. 26.
L. 123.   Luke 12. 20.
L. 137.   Mat. 7. 14.
L. 164.   Rev. 22. 17.
L. 169.   Mat. 7. 13.
L. 176.   Mat. 15. 14.
L. 208.   1 Cor. 15. 20;
L. 210.   Phil. 2. 9.
L. 254.   John 7. 46.
L. 319.   Rom. 8. 28.
L. 283.   Gen. 8. 22.
L. 294.   Rom. 13. 4.
L. 313.   Cant. 2. 10.
L. 329.   Lovely penitent ariſe.   *More.*
L. 356.   1 Theſſ. 2. 19.

NOTES to PART VI.

PREFATORY NOTE I.

THIS part of the poem, though deſigned, in a degree, for perſons in
moſt employments of life, is immediately addreſſed to Farmers. As almoſt
all the inhabitants of Greenfield, and of New England, are farmers, it was
ſuppoſed by the writer, that this circumſtance naturally directed to ſuch an
addreſs.

L. 63.   [Lawrence.] A proverbial name, in ſome parts of New England,
for a lazy perſon.

L. 148.   [Fit the ground.] A cuſtomary phraſe, in ſome parts of New
England, to denote the preparatory cultivation of a field, which is to be
ſown.

L. 270.   It is cuſtomary, in New England, when property is taken by
diſtreſs, to advertiſe the ſale of it upon a poſt, erected for that purpoſe.

L. 289. [The firſt of May.] The day, on w..ich accounts are uſually adjuſted, and pecuniary obligations diſcharged, in the ſtate of New-York.

L. 297. For more than twenty years, the writer of this poem has been employed in the buſineſs of education, and, in that time, has had, in a greater or leſs degree, the ſuperintendence of almoſt a thouſand young perſons, of both ſexes. Almoſt all the ſentiments here expreſſed, concerning the inſtruction, government, and habituation, of children, he has ſeen often proved to be juſt, through the whole courſe of this extenſive experience. He is induced to theſe obſervations by a full, experimental conviction of the entirely theoretical and viſionary nature of ſeveral modern opinions on the ſubject; opinions, publiſhed by men, of genius indeed, but wholly inexperienced in education; men who educate children on paper, as a geometrician circumnavigates the globe, in half a dozen ſpherical triangles. On ſome future occaſion, he may, perhaps, take the liberty to offer to the public ſome further ſentiments, on this copious and very intereſting ſubject. In the mean time, he believes, that theſe may be ſafely adopted by ſuch, as have not acquired more extenſive information, and for ſuch only are they deſigned.

L. 447. No principle of action will uſually be of any ſervice to children, unleſs it be made habitual.

L. 451. I believe, that there are very few children, who might not be rendered amiable and worthy, if their parents would begin their efforts in ſeaſon, and continue them ſteadily, without yielding to either ſloth, or diſcouragement.

L. 471. In moſt places in New England, the pariſh bell is rung, at 9 o'clock, in the evening: a cuſtom, which has more influence in promoting good order, than a ſlight obſerver would imagine.

L. 531. There are many ſocial libraries in Connecticut; and the number is faſt-increaſing. This is viſibly one of the beſt means of diffuſing knowledge. If the proprietors of each would tax themſelves a ſmall ſum yearly, they would ſoon be able to procure a ſufficient number of books, to anſwer every valuable purpoſe of ſuch an inſtitution.

L. 567. I once knew a farmer, who ſteadily did what was called a good day's-work, and yet employed ſeveral hours, every day, in reading.

L. 570. Several of the moſt uſeful and reſpectable men, in America, were privately educated; and ſome of them, with very ſmall advantages.

L. 637. [A townſman.] In New England, the prudentials of each town are commonly placed under the direction of a ſmall number of men, choſen for that purpoſe, and called indifferently ſelectmen or townſmen.

L. 638. A repreſentative; Vulgarly called a member of the houſe.

NOTES to PART VII.

LINE 11. 12. The viſions of the morning were anciently thought to be peculiarly prophetical.

L. 42. [Thames.] The river which empties into the found at New London.

L. 43. [Tempe.] A beautiful valley in Theffaly. [Connecta.[Connecticut river, which, almoft through its whole courfe, waters a very fruitful and delightful valley.

L. 45. [Avon.] Houfatonuck, or, as it ought to be written, Hooeftennuck, or Stratford river.

L. 96. Quicquid delirant reges. plectuntur Achivi. *Horace.*

L. 105. The great objects of nature are, in America, vifibly formed on a fcale, fuperior to what is found elfewhere. Mountains, lakes, plains, cataracts, &c. exift in America, which are wholly unequalled by any, on the Eaftern continent.

L. 113. 114. The Inconveniencies, arifing from the extremes of heat and cold, in N. America, are abundantly compenfated by the great variety and richnefs of its productions. The two harvefts, of European grain, and Indian corn (one of which is almoft always a plentiful one) will probably hereafter, as they have done heretofore, ever forbid even a fcarcity of the neceffaries of life.

125. The foundation of all equal liberty is the natural and equal defcent of property to all the children of the proprietor. Republics cannot long exift, but upon this bafis.

L. 145. A very unequal divifion of property appears ever to have had very baneful effects on the general happinefs of mankind. A great part of the profperity of Great Britain may be attributed to the inroads made by Henry VII. upon the entailment of eftates.

L. 150. Prov. 30. 8, 9.

L. 154. Luke 18. 2.

L. 162. Irreligion and fuperftition are equally confequences of great wealth, ignorance, and power, in perfons of different characters.

L. 165, 166. The vaffals, or loweft clafs of people, were, anciently, in moft European countries, and are, at the prefent time, in fome, fold with the foil.

L. 176. Prov. 30. 9.

L. 183. [Vitellius.] A luxurious emperor of Rome, who had, ferved up for him at one meal, 2000 fifh, and 7000 fowl.

L. 192. [Staniflaus.] The prefent king of Poland. The fate of this prince is exceedingly to be lamented. Having, in a moft dignified manner, made his country free, and laid a moft defirable foundation for it's future happinefs, he was fruftrated, in the nobleft of attempts, by the interference of injuftice and tyranny.

L. 204. Matt 25. 40.

L. 251. In the United States, the world has, for the firft time, feen a nation eftablifhing, diffolving, and renewing, its fyftem of government, with as much peace, order, and coolnefs of deliberation, as commonly appear in the cuftomary bufinefs of a legiflature.

L. 282. Rev. 21. 25.

L. 367. [Calm Main] Pacific ocean.

L. 368. [Hudfon.] Hudfon's bay.

L. 378. By the laws of Great Britain, one hundred and fixty different forts of human actions are punifhable with death. *Blackftone's Com.*

This fact is a dreadful inftance of the aftonifhing power of eftablifhed cuftom, and hereditary opinion: for the nation in which it is found, is unqueftionably the moft enlightened and refpectable, in Europe.

Since Blackstone wrote, Capel Loft estimates the number of felonies, without benefit of Clergy, at 176; and of felonies with Clergy, at 65.— Of those, who were executed, the Solicitor General declares, that 18 out of 20 do not exceed 20 years of age.

L. 386. It has not yet been proved, that the punishment of death can, with either justice, or policy, be inflicted for any other crime, beside murder. From the few experiments, which have been made, solitary confinement appears to be as much more effectual as it is more humane.

The present penal system of Pennsylvania well deserves the respect and the adoption of every Government. To the original authors of this system, among whom several of the Friends claim a particular distinction, the highest honour is due. See, on this subject, An Enquiry how far the punishment of Death is necessary, in Pennsylvania. By William Bradford, esq. And an Account of the Alteration, and present State, of the penal Laws, in Pennsylvania; of the Gaol, &c. By Caleb Lownes.

L. 395, 396. Acts 12. 8. 9.

L. 401. It seems not a little surprising, that almost the whole business of distributive government should, hitherto, have been to punish.

L. 413—416. There is no country, in which law has a more decided; (and if I may be allowed the expression) despotic power, than in Connecticut. Yet this power rests wholly on that general information of the people at large; from which they derive full conviction, that government is necessary to the existence, and to the continuance, of all their happiness.

L. 425. In the sword of the constellation, Orion, there is a place, which appears like a window in the sky; through which the eye apparently penetrating sees, in telescopes of high powers, a more glorious region, than has been elsewhere discovered; a region in which perpetual day seems to shine with singular splendour.

L. 482. [Indian Wind.] The hurricane.

L. 499, 500. Curs'd be the verse, how well so'er it flow,
That tends to make one worthy man my foe;
Give Virtue scandal, Innocence a fear,
Or from the soft-ey'd Virgin steal a tear. *Pope.*

A person of delicacy, and virtue, is naturally led to wonder, that a man of such talents, as Mr. Pope possessed, and entertaining the very just sentiments, expressed in these finished lines, should have written, published, and left to be handed down to posterity, a great number of verses, which he has actually written, and published. In his Rape of the Lock, there are several lines plainly indelicate, and some grossly obscene. In his Eloisa to Abelard, the sentiments are, in some instances, gross and noxious. Yet these are his first performances. His Moral Essays (particularly the second) trespass, at times, against truth, justice and decency. The same is too often true of his satires. The Dunciad is, in several places, a severer satire on the author, than on the objects of his resentment: not to mention several of his smaller imitations of other poets, and the hideous volume, published as a supplement to his acknowledged works.

No Writer ought ever to publish a sentiment, or expression (unless when some scientifical, or other important purpose necessitates it) which cannot be read, in a mixed company, of Ladies and Gentlemen, without giving pain to the most refined and delicate mind.

L. 501, 502. And in our own (excuse some courtly stains)
No whiter page than Addison's remains. *Pope.*

The drummer of Mr. Addifon offends, not unfrequently, againſt decency. There are alſo, in his other works, a few paſſages, which one could wiſh had been expunged. Theſe facts are a proof of unhappy yielding to the taſte of his times, in a man, who was an ornament to human nature. ·

L. 503. It is not a little injurious to the honour of human nature, that the elegant arts of Poetry, Painting, and Muſic, have, in Europe, been ſo often proſtituted to the celebration of vile characters, to the diſplay of ſubjects and ſentiments groſs and pernicious, and to the commemoration of facts, which deeply ſtain the name of man.

L. 535. Infidel philoſophers frequently impeach, and affect to deſpiſe, the evidence of teſtimony. Yet their own reaſonings are generally attended with evidence, and moſt uſually founded on evidence, which, in clearneſs and ſtrength, is far inferior to that of teſtimony : a great part of their ſentiments being mere and trifling hypotheſes.

L. 565. Warton, in his Eſſay on the genius and writings of Pope, obſerves, that mediocrity is the ſituation, moſt favourable to the exertions of genius. It is alſo the ſituation, evidently moſt friendly to national, and individual, virtue and happineſs.

L. 583. · There is ſomething ſingularly unhappy in the attempts of the Americans to imitate the burthenſome oſtentation of Europe. Americans are not, and probably will not ſoon be, ſufficiently acquainted with the round of European form, and etiquette, to adopt it with either ſkill, or grace. At the ſame time, we have not, and, without entailments, never ſhall in any great number of inſtances have, wealth ſufficient to ſupport the neceſſary expenſe.

Common Senſe, Philoſophy, and Religion, alike condemn ſuch manners, in every inſtance, and view them, as the painful efforts of folly to lift itſelf into reſpectability. The plain manners of Republicans, incomparably leſs burthenſome, and more graceful and pleaſing, are our own native manners ſuch manners, as made the Gaul eſteem the Roman ſenate an aſſembly of gods ; and the courtier Cineas conſider the citizens of Rome, as a collection of kings.

Senſible travellers, whoſe manners are generally viewed as more finiſhed and pleaſing, than any other, appear uſually to acquire a contempt, and diſuſe, of ceremony, and to adopt a plainer behaviour, than moſt other men of breeding. A perſevering adoption of plain manners, by men of influence, would give them a general and laſting ſanction ; and prove of more real benefit to the preſent, and future, inhabitants of America, than renowned victories, or immenſe acquiſitions of territory.

It may, perhaps, be ſaid, as it often has been ſaid, though with neither diſcernment, nor truth, that parade is neceſſary to give energy to law, and dignity to government. It may be anſwered, that no laws have greater energy, and no government was ever more reſpected, than thoſe of Connecticut have uſually been, for more than 150 years. Yet in Connecticut, parade is unknown in practice, and deſpiſed by the univerſal opinion.—The truth is, people of mere common ſenſe, and uneducated to ceremony, always deſpiſe it : it's introduction, therefore, is always owing to the vanity, and weakneſs, of men in ſuperior ſtations, or ranks, of life.

L. 597. There is reaſon to believe, that the women, in New England, in all that renders the female character reſpectable, and lovely, are inferior to none, in the world. They blend the uſeful, and the pleaſing, the refined, and the excellent, into a moſt delightful, and dignified union ; and

(183)

well deferve, from the other fex, that high regard, and polite attention,
which form a very refpectable branch of our national manners.

L. 657. One of the greateft improvements, which the prefent age has
made, in the progrefs of fociety, is the public diminution of military glory,
and the elevation of character, acquired by benevolence. Thus Howard
is a name more celebrated, than Cæfar, or Marlborough.

F I N I S.

THE READER IS REQUESTED TO CORRECT THE FOLLOWING ERRORS.

P. 1.	Line	for	read
	95	*wakes*	*awakes*
	172	*very*	*every*
	176	*commands*	*commends*
	241	*his*	*the*
	288	*Bloated*	*Eloated*
	411	*talk*	*task*
	543	after *day* dele ,	

P. II.	L.	for	read
	162	*beggars,*	*beggars'*
	129	*fucking*	*fuckling*
	390	*hardy*	*hardly*
	644	*e'er*	*o'er*
	670	*dun*	*fad*
	717	*Commerce,*	*Commerce'*
	736	*murmurs*	*murmur*

P. III. Argument. laft Line dele *and*

	L.	for	read
	171	*fofter*	*fofteft*
	221	*wary*	*wavy*
	412	*ocean*	*ocean's*
	531	*haunt*	*hunt*
	542	*invok'd*	*invok'd,*

	558	*the*	*thy*
P. IV.	Arg. L. 9. for	*tribes*	*tribe*
	2	*towards*	*toward*
	9	*forrows*	*forrow*
	90	*fhrnuk*	*fhrunk*
	163	*clouds*	*cloud*
	176	*around*	*around',*
	177	*ftrew'd*	*ftrow'd*
	187	*ftrew'd*	*ftrow'd*
	210	*in*	*on*
	291	*afpect,*	*afpect*
	297	GODHEAD,	GODHEAD

P. V.	L. 12.	*others*	*others'*
	137	*ftrait*	*ftraight*

P. VI.	L. 176	*the*	*a*
	215	*wood's*	*woods*
	247	*garden*	*gardens*
	372	*minifter'd*	*minifter'*
	381	*parents*	*parent's*
	452	*leaves*	*leave*

P. VII.	L. 186.	*crofe*	*corfe*
	241	*fabric*	*fabrics*